SAS® Guide to TABULATE Processing

Second Edition

SAS Institute Inc.
SAS Campus Drive
Cary, NC 27513

Holly S. Whittle wrote the *SAS® Guide to TABULATE Processing, Second Edition*. **Marian Saffer** is series editor for the SAS Special Topics Series. **Alan R. Eaton** and **Lynn H. Patrick** were contributing editors. **Marla Z. Hudnell** and **J. Chris Parker** were editors.

The correct bibliographic citation for this manual is as follows: SAS Institute Inc., *SAS® Guide to TABULATE Processing, Second Edition,* Cary, NC: SAS Institute Inc., 1990. 208 pp.

SAS® Guide to TABULATE Processing, Second Edition

Copyright © 1990 by SAS Institute Inc., Cary, NC, USA.

ISBN 1-55544-416-4

1st printing, August 1990
2nd printing, May 1991
3rd printing, January 1992

Note that text corrections may have been made at each printing.

The SAS® System is an integrated system of software providing complete control over data access, management, analysis, and presentation. Base SAS software is the foundation of the SAS System. Products within the SAS System include SAS/ACCESS® SAS/AF® SAS/ASSIST® SAS/CPE® SAS/DMI® SAS/ETS® SAS/FSP® SAS/GRAPH® SAS/IML® SAS/IMS-DL/I® SAS/OR® SAS/QC® SAS/REPLAY-CICS® SAS/SHARE® SAS/STAT® SAS/CALC™ SAS/CONNECT™ SAS/DB2™ SAS/EIS™ SAS/INSIGHT™ SAS/LAB™ SAS/LOOKUP™ SAS/NVISION™ SAS/PH-Clinical™ SAS/SQL-DS™ and SAS/TOOLKIT™ software. Other SAS Institute products are SYSTEM 2000® Data Management Software, with basic SYSTEM 2000, CREATE™ Multi-User™ QueX™ Screen Writer™ and CICS interface software; NeoVisuals® software; JMP® JMP IN® JMP SERVE® and JMP Ahead™ software; SAS/RTERM® software; and the SAS/C® Compiler and the SAS/CX® Compiler. MultiVendor Architecture™ and MVA™ are trademarks of SAS Institute Inc. *SAS Communications*® *SAS Training*® *SAS Views*® the SASware Ballot® and *Observations*™ are published by SAS Institute Inc. All trademarks above are registered trademarks or trademarks of SAS Institute Inc. in the USA and other countries. ® indicates USA registration.

The Institute is a private company devoted to the support and further development of its software and related services.

OS/2® is a registered trademark and SQL™ is a trademark of International Business Machines Corporation.

Other brand and product names are registered trademarks or trademarks of their respective companies.

Contents

Illustrations

Figures

Tables

Credits

Alan R. Eaton developed the TABULATE procedure and supports it in Version 5. **Alan R. Eaton** and **Katherine Ng** support TABULATE in Version 6.

Acknowledgment

The TABULATE procedure was inspired in part by the pioneer software package TPL (Table Producing Language) developed at the Bureau of Labor Statistics.

Preface

About This Book

The *SAS Guide to TABULATE Processing, Second Edition* documents the TABULATE procedure, a powerful tool for producing reports of descriptive statistics in tabular format.

Who can use this book   The TABULATE procedure has many features, ranging from simple to complex. You should understand how SAS programs are organized into DATA and PROC steps and how the DATA step works. With this background, you can begin to create simple tables almost immediately and work up to the more complex ones as your experience and needs grow.

How this book relates to other SAS documentation   The *SAS Guide to TABULATE Processing, Second Edition* is the complete source of information on the TABULATE procedure in Version 5 and Version 6 base SAS software. It includes all information on the TABULATE procedure provided by Chapter 37, "The TABULATE Procedure," in the *SAS Procedures Guide, Version 6, Third Edition*, Chapter 26, "The TABULATE Procedure," in the *SAS Procedures Guide for Personal Computers, Version 6 Edition* and Chapter 49, "The TABULATE Procedure," in the *SAS User's Guide: Basics, Version 5 Edition*, and provides other information not included in these books.

For reference material on the SAS programs shown in this book, you should have access to *SAS Language: Reference, Version 6, First Edition*, the *SAS Language Guide for Personal Computers, Version 6 Edition*, or the *SAS User's Guide: Basics, Version 5 Edition*.

For information on the way the SAS System interacts with your host operating system, you may need access to appropriate manuals and technical reports:

- AOS/VS users: *SAS Companion for the AOS/VS Environment, Version 6, First Edition* or SAS Technical Report P-184, *Using the SAS System, Release 5.18, under AOS/VS*
- CMS users: *SAS Companion for the CMS Environment, Version 6, First Edition* or *SAS Companion for the CMS Operating System, 1986 Edition* for Version 5 users
- MVS users: *SAS Companion for the MVS Environment, Version 6, First Edition* or *SAS Companion for OS Operating Systems and TSO, 1984 Edition* for Version 5 users
- OS/2 users: *SAS Companion for the OS/2 Environment, Version 6, First Edition*
- PRIMOS users: *SAS Companion for the PRIMOS Environment, Version 6, First Edition* or SAS Technical Report P-185, *Using the SAS System, Release 5.18, under PRIMOS*
- VMS users: *SAS Companion for the VMS Environment, Version 6, First Edition* or *SAS Companion for the VMS Operating System, 1986 Edition* and SAS Technical Report P-168, *Changes and Enhancements to the Version 5 SAS System under VMS*
- UNIX users: *SAS Companion for the UNIX Environment and Derivatives, Version 6, First Edition* or SAS Technical Report P-176, *Using the SAS System, Release 6.03 under UNIX Operating Systems and Derivatives*

- VSE users: *SAS Companion for the VSE Operating System, 1987 Edition.*

About This Series

The SAS Special Topics Series includes books of primary documentation and sample applications for topics that require more explanatory detail than is practical to give in a reference guide chapter. Each manual in the series is a complete one-volume usage and reference guide to its subject. Future editions of reference guides will present only basic reference information on topics that are given expanded coverage in the series.

The *SAS Guide to TABULATE Processing, Second Edition* joins the following books in the SAS Special Topics Series:

- *SAS Guide to the SQL Procedure: Usage and Reference, Version 6, First Edition*
- *SAS Guide to Macro Processing, Version 6, Second Edition*
- *SAS Guide to Macro Processing, Version 6, First Edition*
- *SAS Guide to Macro Processing, Version 5 Edition*
- *SAS Guide to the Micro-to-Host Link, Version 6, First Edition*
- *SAS Guide to VSAM Processing, Version 5 Edition*

If You Need Help

If you have questions about the TABULATE procedure that this manual does not answer, please take the time to complete the review page at the end of the book and send it to SAS Institute. We will consider your suggestions for future editions. In the meantime, ask your installation's SAS Software Consultant for help.

INTRODUCTION

Introduction to the TABULATE Procedure

Chapter 1
Introduction to the TABULATE Procedure

To help you use this book, this chapter explains what you will find in the rest of the book and guides you to the parts of the book that are most appropriate for your level of expertise.

Recommended Use

All users: read this chapter for an overview of what this book provides and how to use the book.

Contents

WHAT IS THE TABULATE PROCEDURE?

PROC TABULATE is one of the descriptive procedures in base SAS software. It summarizes values for all observations in a data set and prints the summaries in table format. PROC TABULATE can produce tables with one to three dimensions, and within each dimension it allows multiple variables to be reported one after another or hierarchically.

For example, the rows of the sample table in **Output 1.1** show a hierarchical relationship between accounts and departments in a company. The columns of the sample table show a list of detailed monthly expenditures followed by a summary of total expenditures to-date in the same dimension of the table.

Output 1.1   Sample Table Produced by PROC TABULATE

```
|                            |          |         Monthly Expenditures            |           |
|                            |          |------------------------------------------|           |
|                            |          | JANUARY  |  FEBRUARY  |   MARCH    |   Total   |
|----------------------------+----------+----------+------------+------------+-----------|
|Department      |Account    |          |          |            |            |           |
|----------------+-----------|          |          |            |            |           |
|ACCOUNTING      |1345       |  38,088.00|  93,341.00|  103,587.00|  235,016.00|
|                |-----------+-----------+-----------+------------+------------|
|                |1578       |  23,476.00|  23,182.00|   13,205.00|   59,863.00|
|                |-----------+-----------+-----------+------------+------------|
|                |1674       |  35,065.00|  39,713.00|   64,089.00|  138,867.00|
|                |-----------+-----------+-----------+------------+------------|
|                |Sub-Total  |  96,629.00| 156,236.00|  180,881.00|  433,746.00|
|----------------+-----------+-----------+-----------+------------+------------|
|HUMAN RESOURCES |Account    |          |          |            |            |
|                |-----------|          |          |            |            |
|                |2134       | 101,297.00|  77,938.00|   71,598.00|  250,833.00|
|                |-----------+-----------+-----------+------------+------------|
|                |2403       |  74,722.00|  49,811.00|   29,369.00|  153,902.00|
|                |-----------+-----------+-----------+------------+------------|
|                |Sub-Total  | 176,019.00| 127,749.00|  100,967.00|  404,735.00|
|----------------+-----------+-----------+-----------+------------+------------|
|SYSTEMS         |Account    |          |          |            |            |
|                |-----------|          |          |            |            |
|                |4138       |  72,920.00|  66,111.00|  120,286.00|  259,317.00|
|                |-----------+-----------+-----------+------------+------------|
|                |4279       |  29,297.00|  41,694.00|   39,615.00|  110,606.00|
|                |-----------+-----------+-----------+------------+------------|
|                |4290       |  32,126.00|  42,663.00|   33,626.00|  108,415.00|
|                |-----------+-----------+-----------+------------+------------|
|                |Sub-Total  | 134,343.00| 150,468.00|  193,527.00|  478,338.00|
|----------------+-----------+-----------+-----------+------------+------------|
|Total                       | 406,991.00| 434,453.00|  475,375.00|1,316,819.00|
```

BEYOND BASICS: WHAT THIS BOOK PROVIDES

This manual provides all of the information about PROC TABULATE that is given in the *SAS User's Guide: Basics, Version 5 Edition* and the *SAS Procedures Guide for Personal Computers, Version 6 Edition* and also includes

- tutorials on how to use PROC TABULATE
- extended sample applications
- details of internal processing.

This guide serves a wide range of audiences, from the first-time TABULATE user to the experienced user who wants more details on how features of TABULATE interact.

How to Use This Book

If you have seldom or never used PROC TABULATE, carefully read the two tutorial chapters, "Learning to Use PROC TABULATE" and "Controlling the Table's Appearance," and skim Chapter 2, "TABULATE Procedure Description," to get a sense of the organization of the TABULATE procedure. As you become more familiar with PROC TABULATE, you may want to read Chapter 3, "Details of TABULATE Processing."

Advanced users will want to read Chapter 3 and selected topics in Chapters 4 and 5. Chapter 2 provides a brief summary of the statements and options available with the TABULATE procedure. The sample applications chapters, "Public Health Clinic Example" and "A Multiple-Response Example," will help even advanced users improve their coding techniques.

Chapter and Appendix Descriptions

The following paragraphs describe each chapter and appendix in this guide to help you select the ones you need to read.

This chapter, "Introduction to the TABULATE Procedure," provides a general overview of the book and how it can assist you in effectively using PROC TABULATE.

Chapter 2, "TABULATE Procedure Description," is the primary reference description of PROC TABULATE. This section provides a brief summary of the statements and options available with the TABULATE procedure.

Chapter 3, "Details of TABULATE Processing," provides detailed information on how TABULATE processes data to produce tables. This chapter describes how TABULATE organizes data, handles missing values, and calculates percentages. In addition, information on estimating resources is provided to help advanced users fine-tune their PROC TABULATE applications.

Chapter 4, "Learning to Use PROC TABULATE," is a tutorial on how to write TABLE statements to produce the tables you want. This chapter explains the dimensions of the table, what it means to cross and concatenate variables, and how to calculate percentages with PROC TABULATE.

Chapter 5, "Controlling the Table's Appearance," is also a tutorial, but this chapter focuses exclusively on how to format output from PROC TABULATE. Detailed discussions provide methods for tailoring page, row, and column headings, formatting values printed in the table cells, and changing the characters used to outline the table.

Chapter 6, "Public Health Clinic Example," illustrates several uses of PROC TABULATE in the context of a public health clinic. The coding techniques in this chapter are generally applicable to many industry needs, not only those of the health care industry.

Chapter 7, "A Multiple-Response Example," illustrates how to handle the data generated by a multiple-response survey and produce reports with PROC TABULATE.

Appendix 1, "Glossary," lists terms and definitions as they are used in this guide. If you encounter terminology in this book that is not familiar to you, refer to the glossary.

Appendix 2, "Answers to Common Questions," describes some questions that users commonly ask and provides suggestions for handling these situations.

PREREQUISITES

In order to use PROC TABULATE and this book, you need a basic knowledge of the SAS DATA step language and a general understanding of SAS variables and SAS data sets.

CONVENTIONS

The examples used throughout this book to illustrate coding techniques are run using the following OPTIONS and TITLE statements:

```
OPTIONS NOCENTER NODATE NONUMBER;
TITLE;
```

All tables labeled as **Figures** are run with the LINESIZE= option set to 64. Tables labeled as **Output** are run with LINESIZE=120.

Figures illustrate detailed techniques discussed in the text. Some figures have portions of the output removed to emphasize the portion that is being discussed. **Output** is used only to illustrate complete tables that are produced by combining a number of coding techniques.

Color is used throughout the book to provide emphasis to important topics. Colored text in the narrative highlights the first use of words defined in the glossary. Colored text in the examples emphasizes coding techniques. Colored outlining boxes highlight summary material so that you can easily find it for quick reference.

8

REFERENCE

TABULATE Procedure Description

Details of TABULATE Processing

Chapter 2
TABULATE
Procedure
Description

PROC TABULATE constructs tables of descriptive statistics from class variables, analysis variables, and keywords for statistics. Tables can have one to three dimensions: column; row and column; or page, row, and column. This chapter briefly describes the TABULATE procedure. Detailed information on topics introduced in this chapter can be found in the remainder of the book.

Recommended Use

New users: skim this chapter to get an overview of all statements in the TABULATE procedure.

Experienced users: use this chapter as a reference to refresh your memory with the statements and options in the TABULATE procedure.

Contents

INTRODUCTION

The TABULATE procedure displays descriptive statistics in tabular format. The value in each table cell is calculated from the variables and statistics that define the pages, rows, and columns of the table. The statistic associated with each cell is calculated on values from all observations in that category. PROC TABULATE computes many of the same statistics that are computed by other descriptive statistical procedures such as MEANS, FREQ, and SUMMARY. PROC TABULATE provides

- simple but powerful methods to create tabular reports
- flexibility in classifying the values of variables and establishing hierarchical relationships between the variables
- mechanisms for labeling and formatting variables and procedure-generated statistics.

SPECIFICATIONS

The TABULATE procedure is controlled by the following statements:

PROC TABULATE <*option-list*>;
   CLASS *class-variable-list*;
   VAR *analysis-variable-list*;
   TABLE<<*page-expression,*> *row-expression,*> *column-expression*
      </ *table-option-list*>;
   BY <NOTSORTED> <DESCENDING> *variable-1*
      <...<DESCENDING> *variable-n*>;
   FORMAT *variable-list-1 format-1* <...*variable-list-n format-n*>;
   FREQ *variable*;
   KEYLABEL *keyword-1*='*description-1*' <...*keyword-n*='*description-n*'>;
   LABEL *variable-1*='*label-1*' <...*variable-n*='*label-n*'>;
   WEIGHT *variable*;

The PROC TABULATE statement is always accompanied by one or more TABLE statements specifying the tables to be produced. In addition, you must use either a VAR statement or a CLASS statement or both. All variables used in the TABLE statement must be specified in either the VAR statement or the CLASS statement, but not both. The WEIGHT, FREQ, and BY statements are optional; each can be specified once for the entire TABULATE procedure step. The FORMAT, LABEL, and KEYLABEL statements are also optional; if you repeat one of these statements, the value in the last statement applies to the entire step.

PROC TABULATE Statement

PROC TABULATE <*option-list*>;

You can specify the following options in the PROC TABULATE statement:

DATA=*SAS-data-set*
   specifies the SAS data set used by PROC TABULATE. If you omit the DATA= option, PROC TABULATE uses the SAS data set created most recently in the current job or session.

DEPTH=*number*
   specifies the maximum depth of any dimension's crossing. (Refer to **TABLE Statement** later in this chapter for an explanation of crossings.) The default depth is 10. You may need to increase the value for the

(continued on next page)

SPECIFICATIONS

(continued from previous page)

DEPTH= option, but there is no benefit to decreasing the value. The depth of a crossing refers to the number of elements, including the default statistic, that are crossed with each other within any single dimension of the TABLE statement. For example, the depth of the following TABLE statement is 3 because the default statistic must be included in the crossing:

```
table a*b;
```

Note: Format modifiers are also counted in the crossings. Therefore, the maximum depth of the following TABLE statement is 5:

```
table a*b,x*y*z*sum*f=10.0;
```

FORMAT=_format-name_
specifies a default format for formatting the value in each table cell. You can use any valid SAS or user-defined format. If you omit the FORMAT= option, PROC TABULATE uses BEST12.2 as the default format. The default format is overridden by any formats specified in a TABLE statement. This option is especially useful for decreasing the number of print positions used to print a table. Refer to Chapter 5, "Controlling the Table's Appearance," for more information on formatting output.

FORMCHAR<(_index-list_)>='_string_'
FC<(_index-list_)>='_string_'
defines the characters used for constructing the table outlines and dividers. The value is a string 11 characters long defining the two bar characters, vertical and horizontal, and the 9 corner characters: upper left, upper middle, upper right, middle left, middle middle (cross), middle right, lower left, lower middle, and lower right. The default value is FORMCHAR= '|----|+|---'. You can substitute any character or hexadecimal string to customize the table's appearance. You can replace the entire default string by specifying a full 11-character replacement string, or you can replace selected characters by including an index list that indicates which characters are to be replaced. For example, change the four corners to asterisks by using

```
FORMCHAR(3 5 9 11)= '****'
```

Specifying 11 blanks produces tables with blank outlines and dividers:

```
FORMCHAR='
```

Refer to Chapter 5 for more information on formatting output.

MISSING
considers missing values as valid levels for the class variables. Special missing values are considered as different level values.* A heading for each missing value is shown in the table. Unless the MISSING option is specified, PROC TABULATE does not include observations with a missing value for one or more class variables in the analysis.

(continued on next page)

---

* Special missing values are the uppercase letters A through Z and the underscore (_), which are used to represent missing *numeric* values. Refer to **Missing Values with Special Meanings** in Chapter 2, "The DATA Step," in *SAS Language: Reference, Version 6, First Edition* for more information.

SPECIFICATIONS

(continued from previous page)

NOSEPS
eliminates horizontal separator lines from the row titles and body of the printed table. Horizontal separator lines remain in the column title section of the table. Note that the NOSEPS option completely removes the separator lines instead of substituting blank characters, as illustrated in the FORMCHAR= option discussed earlier in this chapter.

ORDER=order
specifies the order in which headings for class variable values are displayed in each table. Specifying ORDER=DATA keeps values of class variables in the order they were encountered when the input was read. Note that the order remains the same for the entire data set or BY group if a BY statement is specified.
Specifying ORDER=FORMATTED orders the class values by the formatted (external) representation of the value.
Specifying ORDER=FREQ orders the headings for class variables by descending frequency count so that class values occurring in the greatest number of observations come first.
Specifying ORDER=INTERNAL orders the headings in the same sequence as they would be ordered by the SORT procedure.
If you omit the ORDER= option, PROC TABULATE defaults to ORDER=INTERNAL.

VARDEF=divisor
specifies the divisor to be used in the calculation of the variances. If divisor is DF, the degrees of freedom (N−1) is used as the divisor. If divisor is N, the number of observations (N) is used. If divisor is WDF, the sum of the weights minus one is used. If divisor is WEIGHT or WGT, the sum of the weights is used. The default is VARDEF=DF.

BY Statement

BY <NOTSORTED> <DESCENDING> variable-1
<...<DESCENDING> variable-n>;

Use a BY statement with PROC TABULATE to obtain separate analyses on observations in groups defined by the BY variables.

Note that the page-dimension expression of a TABLE statement can have an effect similar to using a BY statement. Your input data set need not be sorted or indexed when the page-dimension expression is used. The page dimension should be used in most cases where a new page is desired for a given level of a class variable or combination of variables. Refer to **TABLE Statement** later in this chapter for more information on the page dimension and **Comparison of BY-Group Processing to Using the Page Dimension** in Chapter 3, "Details of TABULATE Processing."

When a BY statement appears, the TABULATE procedure expects the input data set to be sorted in order of the BY variables or to have an appropriate index. If your input data set is not sorted in ascending order, you can do one of the following:

* Remove the BY statement and use the page dimension to produce the same effect as the BY statement.

(continued on next page)

SPECIFICATIONS

(continued from previous page)

- Use the SORT procedure with a similar BY statement to sort the data.
- If appropriate, use the BY statement options NOTSORTED or DESCENDING.
- Create an index on the BY variables you want to use. For more information on indexes, see Chapter 17, "The DATASETS Procedure" in *SAS Procedures Guide, Version 6, Third Edition.*

The following options can be specified in the BY statement:

DESCENDING
> specifies that the data set is sorted in descending order by the variable that immediately follows the word DESCENDING in the BY statement.

NOTSORTED
> specifies that observations are not necessarily sorted in alphabetic or numeric order. This option can appear anywhere in the BY statement.

CLASS Statement

> **CLASS** *class-variable-list*;
> **CLASSES** *class-variable-list*;

Use the CLASS statement to identify variables in the input data set as class variables. Class variables may have either numeric or character values. Normally each class variable has a small number of discrete values or unique levels. Continuous values for a numeric variable can be grouped into discrete levels by using the FORMAT procedure and then including a FORMAT statement in the PROC TABULATE step. Refer to Chapter 3 for more information on creating classes.

If an observation contains missing values for any variable listed in the CLASS statement, the observation is not included in the table unless you specify the MISSING option in the PROC TABULATE statement. Note that the variables listed in the CLASS statement affect observations regardless of whether the class variable appears in a TABLE statement because the CLASS statement is in effect for the entire PROC TABULATE step.

FORMAT Statement

> **FORMAT** *variable-list-1 format-1* <*...variable-list-n format-n*>;

where

> *variable-list*   names one or more variables to format.
>
> *format*   specifies the format for the preceding variables.

In the TABULATE procedure, the FORMAT statement formats the values of class variables used as headings in the page, row, and column dimensions. The FORMAT statement has no effect on either analysis variables (variables specified in the VAR statement) or the content of table cells.

You can use the FORMAT statement in combination with the FORMAT procedure to group values of class variables. Keep in mind that when you use PROC FORMAT to define temporary user-written formats, you must also use the

(continued on next page)

SPECIFICATIONS

(continued from previous page)

FORMAT statement in the PROC TABULATE step to associate the format with the variable.* Refer to **Setting Up Useful Classes** in Chapter 3 for more information on how to use the FORMAT statement and PROC FORMAT.

FREQ Statement

FREQ *variable;*

The FREQ statement specifies a numeric variable in the input SAS data set whose value represents the frequency of the observation.

If you use the FREQ statement, each observation in the input data set is assumed to represent *n* observations, where *n* is the value of the FREQ variable. If the value is not an integer, the value is truncated to the integer portion. If the FREQ variable has a value less than 1, PROC TABULATE skips the observation. You can use only one variable in a FREQ statement. The FREQ statement can be used in combination with the WEIGHT statement.

KEYLABEL Statement

KEYLABEL *keyword-1='label-1' <...keyword-n='label-n'>;*

where

    keyword is one of the valid keywords for statistics discussed in **STATISTICS AVAILABLE WITH PROC TABULATE** later in this chapter, or the universal class variable ALL (discussed in **TABLE Statement** later in this chapter).

    label is up to 40 characters of labeling information. The *label* must be enclosed in single or double quotes.

PROC TABULATE uses the replacement text in the label anywhere the specified keyword is used, unless another label is assigned in the TABLE statement. The KEYLABEL statement is useful for relabeling a keyword once in a PROC TABULATE step rather than each time it occurs in a TABLE statement. Each keyword can have only one label in a particular PROC TABULATE step; if you request multiple labels for the same keyword, PROC TABULATE uses the last one specified in the step. An example of a KEYLABEL statement is

```
keylabel all='Total $'
         mean='Average'
         pctsum='Percent of Sum';
```

LABEL Statement

LABEL *variable-1='label-1' <...variable-n='label-n'>;*

where

    variable names a class or analysis variable used in a TABLE statement.

(continued on next page)

---

* You can also create permanent formats by assigning the format in a DATA step. In this case, you do not need the FORMAT statement in the PROC TABULATE step.

┌───

SPECIFICATIONS ──────────────────

(continued from previous page)

> *label* specifies a label of up to 40 characters, including blanks, for the variable. The *label* must be enclosed in single or double quotes.

The label specified for the variable replaces the name of the variable in the page, row, or column heading where the variable appears. Any number of pairs of variable names and labels can be specified in a LABEL statement.

TABLE Statement

> **TABLE** <<*page-expression,*> *row-expression,*> *column-expression* </ *table-option-list*>;

The TABLE statement describes the table to be printed. Every PROC TABULATE step requires at least one TABLE statement. All variables used in the TABLE statement must be specified in either the VAR statement or the CLASS statement but not both.

A TABLE statement consists of one to three dimension expressions separated by commas that can be followed by an option list. If all three dimensions are specified, the leftmost dimension defines pages, the middle dimension defines rows, and the rightmost dimension defines columns. If two dimensions are specified, the left defines rows, and the right defines columns. If a single dimension is specified, it defines columns.

The *page-expression*, *row-expression*, and *column-expression* are constructed in the same way and are referred to collectively as *dimension expressions*. A dimension expression is composed of elements and operators.

The elements you can use in a dimension expression are

- analysis variables. Refer to **VAR Statement** later in this chapter for more information.
- class variables. Refer to **CLASS Statement** earlier in this chapter for more information.
- the universal class variable ALL, which summarizes all of the categories for class variables in the same parenthetical group or dimension (if the variable ALL is not contained in a parenthetical group).
- keywords for statistics. Refer to **STATISTICS AVAILABLE WITH PROC TABULATE** later in this chapter for more information.
- format modifiers, which define how to format values in cells. These have the form f=*format* and must be crossed with the elements that produce the cells you want to format. See Chapter 5 for more information.
- labels, which temporarily replace the names of variables and statistics with a label. These have the form =*'label'* and affect only the variable or statistic that immediately precedes the label.
- expressions formed by combining any of these elements.

A dimension expression can have any of the following forms:

*element*element*	(crossing)
element element	(concatenation)
(*element element*)	(grouping)

(continued on next page)

SPECIFICATIONS

(continued from previous page)

When you cross class variables in an expression, PROC TABULATE creates categories from the combination of values of the variables. If one of the elements in the crossing is an analysis variable, the statistics for the analysis variable are calculated for the categories created by the class variables.

Concatenating elements joins information for the elements by placing the output for the second element immediately after the output for the first element.

Grouping elements causes the operator adjacent to the parenthesis to be applied to each concatenated element inside the parentheses.

Table 2.1 lists the operators and the effects they produce.

Table 2.1   Effects of Operators in the TABLE Statement

Operator		Action
,	(comma)	separates dimensions of a table and crosses elements across dimensions
*	(asterisk)	crosses elements within a dimension
	(blank space)	concatenates elements in a dimension
()	(parentheses)	group elements and associate an operator with an entire group
<>	(brackets)	specify denominator definitions
=	(equal sign)	assigns a label to a variable or statistic, or completes a format modifier

A TABLE statement can define only one table. Multiple TABLE statements can appear in one PROC TABULATE step, each defining a separate table. Refer to Chapter 4, "Learning to Use PROC TABULATE," for more information on dimension expressions and how to construct TABLE statements.

You can use the following options in the TABLE statement:

BOX=*value*
   specifies the text to be placed in the empty box above the row titles. When BOX=_PAGE_, the page-dimension text appears in the box. If the page-dimension text does not fit, it is placed in its default position, and the box is left empty.
   When BOX='*string*', the quoted string appears in the box. Any name, label, or quoted string that does not fit is truncated.
   When BOX=*variable*, the name or label of a variable appears in the box.

CONDENSE
   prints multiple logical pages on a single physical page. PROC TABULATE prints as many complete logical pages as fit on a single printed page. This option can be used to condense multiple pages generated by the page dimension of the TABLE statement, or multiple pages caused by tables that are too wide to fit on a single page. The CONDENSE option has no effect on the pages generated by the BY statement.

(continued on next page)

SPECIFICATIONS

(continued from previous page)

FUZZ=*number*
> supplies a numeric value against which analysis variable values and table cell values other than frequency counts are compared to eliminate trivial values (absolute values less than the FUZZ= value) from computation and printing. A number whose absolute value is less than the FUZZ= value is treated as zero in computations and printing. The default value is the smallest representable floating-point number on the computer you are using.

MISSTEXT='*text*'
> supplies up to 20 characters of text to print in table cells containing missing values.

PRINTMISS
> specifies that row and column headings are the same for all logical pages of the table. The PRINTMISS option indicates that you want to print all values that occur for a class variable each time headings for that variable are printed. For example, consider a data set with the three observations below:

> A   B

> 1   1
> 3   1
> 3   3

> The following TABLE statement does not produce a column for A=1 and B=3 because this combination does not exist in the data set:

> ```
>     table a*b;
> ```

> If you specify the PRINTMISS option, the table includes a column for A=1 and B=3 with missing values for all table cells in the column.
>   If an entire logical page contains only missing values, that page does not print regardless of the PRINTMISS option. Note: By default PROC TABULATE does not suppress a row or column with all missing values when the missing values are the result of computations on analysis variables. The PRINTMISS option affects only missing rows and columns that result from combinations of class variable values that do not exist.

ROW=*spacing*
> specifies whether all title elements in a row crossing are allotted space even when they are blank. When ROW=CONSTANT or CONST, all row title elements have space allotted to them, even if the title has been blanked out (for example, N=' ' in the row dimension). CONSTANT is the default. When ROW=FLOAT, the row title space is divided equally among the nonblank title elements in the crossing.

RTSPACE=*number*
RTS=*number*
> supplies an integer value that specifies the number of print positions allotted to the headings in the row dimension. Note that this space is divided equally among all levels of row headings and includes spaces used to print outlining characters for the row headings. The default value is one-fourth of the LINESIZE= value. Refer to Chapter 5 for more information on controlling the row title space.

(continued on next page)

SPECIFICATIONS

(continued from previous page)

VAR Statement

VAR *analysis-variable-list*;
VARIABLES *analysis-variable-list*;

Use the VAR statement to identify analysis variables in the input data set. Analysis variables must be numeric and can contain continuous values.

   If an observation contains missing values for a variable listed in the VAR statement, the value is omitted from calculations of all statistics except N (the number of observations with nonmissing variable values) and NMISS (the number of observations with missing variable values). For example, the missing value does not increase the SUM, and it is not counted when calculating statistics such as the MEAN.

WEIGHT Statement

WEIGHT *variable*;
WGT *variable*;

The WEIGHT statement specifies a numeric variable in the input data set whose value is used to weight each analysis variable. Note that the WEIGHT variable value need not be an integer and does not affect the degrees of freedom.

   If you specify a WEIGHT statement, PROC TABULATE uses the value of the WEIGHT variable to calculate weighted statistics. Refer to w_i in the formulas in **STATISTICS AVAILABLE WITH PROC TABULATE** for information on how the WEIGHT value affects statistic calculations.

STATISTICS AVAILABLE WITH PROC TABULATE

A standardized set of keywords is used to refer to the descriptive statistics for PROC TABULATE. Use these keywords to request statistics in the TABLE statement. If a variable name (class or analysis) and a statistic name are the same, specify the statistic name in single quotes.

Keywords and Formulas

The following notations are used where summation is over all nonmissing values:

x_i the ith nonmissing observation of the variable

w_i the weight associated with x_i if a WEIGHT statement is specified, otherwise 1

n the number of nonmissing observations

$\bar{x}$ $= \Sigma w_i x_i / \Sigma w_i$

d $= n$ (if the option VARDEF=N is specified)

    $= n - 1$ (if VARDEF=DF)

    $= \Sigma w_i$ (if VARDEF=WEIGHT or WGT)

    $= \Sigma w_i - 1$ (if VARDEF=WDF)

(continued on next page)

STATISTICS AVAILABLE WITH PROC TABULATE

(continued from previous page)

$$s^2 = \Sigma w_i(x_i - \bar{x})^2/d$$
$$s = \sqrt{s^2}$$
$$z_i = (x_i - \bar{x})/s, \text{ standardized variables.}$$

The formulas and standard keywords for each statistic are given below. In some formulas a keyword is used to designate the corresponding statistic. Refer to the previous notation for an explanation of the symbols used in these formulas.

CSS	$\Sigma w_i(x_i - \bar{x})^2$, the sum of squares corrected for the mean
CV	$100s/\bar{x}$, the percent coefficient of variation
MAX	the maximum value
MEAN	$\bar{x}$, the arithmetic mean
MIN	the minimum value
N	the number of observations with nonmissing variable values
NMISS	the number of observations with missing variable values
PCTN	the percentage that one frequency represents of another frequency
PCTSUM	the percentage that one sum represents of another sum
PRT	the two-tailed p-value for Student's t with $n-1$ degrees of freedom, the probability under the null hypothesis of obtaining an absolute value of t greater than the t value observed in this sample
RANGE	$MAX-MIN$, the range
STD	s, the standard deviation
STDERR	$s/\sqrt{(n)}$, the standard error of the mean
SUM	$\Sigma w_i x_i$, the weighted sum
SUMWGT	Σw_i, the sum of weights
USS	$\Sigma w_i x_i^2$, the uncorrected sum of squares
T	$t=\bar{x}\sqrt{(n)}/s$, Student's t for H_0: population mean$=0$
VAR	s^2, the variance.

Computational Requirements for Statistics

The following requirements are computational requirements and do not describe recommended sample sizes. Statistics are reported as missing if they cannot be computed. The specific requirements for statistics follow:

- N and NMISS do not require any nonmissing observations.
- SUM, MEAN, MAX, MIN, RANGE, USS, and CSS require at least one nonmissing observation.
- VAR, STD, STDERR, CV, T, and PRT require at least two observations.
- T and PRT require that STD is greater than zero.
- CV requires that MEAN is not equal to zero.

Chapter 3

Details of TABULATE Processing

You may find using PROC TABULATE easier if you understand how the procedure handles data from the input data set. This chapter discusses some of the internal processing that occurs as TABULATE builds tables. Two topics of particular interest in this chapter are the discussion of class and analysis variables and the comparison of BY-group processing to PROC TABULATE page dimensions.

Recommended Use

New users: skip this chapter when you are first learning to use PROC TABULATE. Later, you can refer to specific topics for more detailed information on the TABULATE procedure.

Experienced users: select specific topics or read the entire chapter for more detailed information about fine-tuning your use of the TABULATE procedure.

Contents

Figures

HOW PROC TABULATE HANDLES DATA

PROC TABULATE treats the values of variables used to create a table in one of two ways: as discrete classifications of data (class variables) or as continuous values for which you can request descriptive statistics (analysis variables). When you use PROC TABULATE, you indicate how to treat each variable that is used in a TABLE statement by naming the variable in either a VAR statement (for analysis variables) or a CLASS statement (for class variables).

TABULATE uses analysis variables and class variables differently in creating tables. TABULATE constructs categories from the values of class variables and counts the frequency with which each category occurs. For analysis variables, TABULATE uses the value of the variable from each observation and calculates the sum, the mean, or other requested statistics. When class variables are crossed with an analysis variable, TABULATE calculates statistics on the analysis variable for each category.

Analysis variables and class variables are discussed in detail in this section.

Class Variables

The term class variable is used in the context of PROC TABULATE to mean any variable, numeric or character, that you want to use to classify your data into groups or categories of information. Class variables can have character, integer, or even decimal values, but the number of unique values should be limited. Frequently variables in a data set have discrete values, but there are so many different values that any breakdown by these values is meaningless. For example, if you are analyzing data by income levels, your input data set may contain integer values for yearly income, but there are still too many unique income values to be manageable. You can reduce the number of classes by formatting ranges of income into several income levels. Methods for setting up groups of data are discussed in detail in **Setting Up Useful Classes**.

How PROC TABULATE creates categories

To understand how TABULATE summarizes observations by categories or groups, you must understand the concept of crossing variables. A TABLE statement that crosses two or more class variables tells TABULATE to examine the interactions of the values of the class variables.† Each time TABULATE encounters an observation in the data set that has a new combination of values for the crossed class variables, it sets up a category. All subsequent observations with the same combination of values are summarized in this category.

The following example illustrates the categories created for two class variables crossed in the column dimension:

```
DATA SAMPLE;
   INPUT @1 SEX $ @3 RACE $ @5 MARISTAT $;
   CARDS;
F W M
F W S
F B M
M B M
F W S
M B M
```

---

† How to define crossings in a TABLE statement is discussed in Chapter 4, "Learning to Use PROC TABULATE."

```
M B S
F B S
;
PROC TABULATE DATA=SAMPLE;
    CLASS SEX RACE;
    TABLE SEX*RACE;
RUN;
```

For this data set, PROC TABULATE finds three different interactions of values and so creates three categories. Note that because no observations exist that have SEX=M and RACE=W, TABULATE does not create a category for this combination of values.

SEX=F RACE=B
SEX=F RACE=W
SEX=M RACE=B

TABULATE represents these categories in the output table with the headings illustrated in **Figure 3.1**.†

```
------------------------------
|            SEX             |
|---------------------------|
|         F        |   M    |
|------------------+--------|
|       RACE       |  RACE  |
|------------------+--------|
|   B   |    W     |   B    |
|-------+----------+--------|
|   N   |    N     |   N    |
|-------+----------+--------|
```

Figure 3.1 Category Headings in a One-Dimensional Table

Categories are created for the interaction of class variables in different dimensions of the TABLE statement as well as for the values of class variables crossed in the same dimension. Thus, if we use the same data set and these statements:

```
PROC TABULATE DATA=SAMPLE;
    CLASS SEX RACE MARISTAT;
    TABLE SEX,RACE*MARISTAT;
RUN;
```

TABULATE constructs the following categories:‡

SEX=F RACE=B MARISTAT=M
SEX=F RACE=B MARISTAT=S
SEX=F RACE=W MARISTAT=M
SEX=F RACE=W MARISTAT=S
SEX=M RACE=B MARISTAT=M
SEX=M RACE=B MARISTAT=S

The headings created by this TABLE statement are illustrated in **Figure 3.2**.

---

† In some sections of this chapter, portions of the tables produced by TABULATE are removed to emphasize the portions that are being discussed.

‡ As noted before, TABULATE creates categories only for the combinations of values that exist in the data set. The combinations SEX=M RACE=W MARISTAT=S, and SEX=M RACE=W MARISTAT=M do not exist in the data set so there are no categories for them.

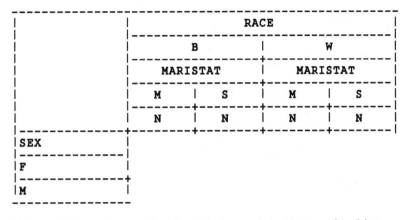

Figure 3.2   Category Headings in a Two-Dimensional Table

Class variables in output

PROC TABULATE orders the pages, rows, and columns of the tables it produces by the values of the class variables. TABULATE uses the same ordering sequence as PROC SORT. Thus, if the variables, SEX and MARISTAT, have the values F and M, and M and S respectively, this TABLE statement

```
TABLE SEX*MARISTAT;
```

produces the headings in **Figure 3.3**.

```
-------------------------------------------------
|                      SEX                      |
|-----------------------------------------------|
|           F            |           M          |
|------------------------+----------------------|
|      MARISTAT          |      MARISTAT         |
|------------------------+----------------------|
|    M    |    S    |    M    |    S    |
|---------+---------+---------+---------|
|    N    |    N    |    N    |    N    |
|---------+---------+---------+---------|
```

Figure 3.3   Default Order of Values for Class Variables

As you can see from **Figure 3.3**, when these two variables are crossed in the same dimension, TABULATE prints all values for class variable MARISTAT within each value for class variable SEX. Note also that all of the headings in this figure are in ascending order of the values of the class variables.

By default, the output table is ordered by the lowest value in a class even when formatted values are used to create classes.† This may cause confusion if you are

---

† Refer to **Modifying the Order of Class Variable Values** for information on changing the default order.

not aware of how classes are ordered. For example, if you have a variable with the following values:

Actual Value	Formatted Value
S	Divorced and Single
M	Married

the order in which these values occur in a table is

Married   Divorced and Single

because by default, the actual value is used for ordering, not the formatted value.

If a class variable is formatted so that a range of values is grouped in one class, TABULATE uses the lowest value in the class as the internal identifier for the class. This can be particularly confusing if one of the groups of values contains a missing value.

For example, consider the formats in the table below. Assume that the values in the column on the left have the format shown in the column on the right.†

Range of Values	Format
0–9999	UNDER 10,000
10000–19999	10,000–19,999
20000–29999	20,000–29,999
30000–39999	30,000–39,999
OTHER	40,000 AND OVER

These formatted values might appear to be ordered the same as the actual values are, but when the formatted values are used in a PROC TABULATE step, a problem occurs.

```
PROC TABULATE FORMAT=8. MISSING;
   CLASS INCOME;
   FORMAT INCOME INCFMT.;
   TABLE INCOME;
RUN;
```

Figure 3.4 illustrates that the internal values have caused the headings to appear in an unexpected order.

```
-------------------------------------------------------
|                        INCOME                       |
|-----------------------------------------------------|
| 40,000 | UNDER  |10,000 -|20,000 -|30,000 -|
|AND OVER| 10,000 | 19,999 | 29,999 | 39,999 |
|--------+--------+--------+--------+--------|
|   N    |   N    |   N    |   N    |   N    |
|--------+--------+--------+--------+--------|
```

Figure 3.4   Unexpected Order of Formatted Headings

---

† The coding required to set up these formats is explained in **Formatting variables into classes**.

Because the MISSING option is specified in the PROC TABULATE statement and no value is specifically stated for missing values, the OTHER category includes missing values. Missing values are lower than numeric values in sorting order. Because the lowest value in the OTHER category is now lower than any value in any other category, the headings in the table have the 40,000 AND OVER class listed before the UNDER 10,000 class. To maintain a reasonable order for the headings, use the code that produces **Figure 3.5** and separate the missing values from the high numbers. Also refer to **Modifying the Order of Class Variable Values** for information on overriding the default order.

Setting Up Useful Classes

The major determining factor for creating good class variables is whether the report produced by PROC TABULATE is useful and meaningful. In some cases, you may have a class variable in the page dimension that has 100 unique values and all 100 pages of the report are useful. In many cases, however, you can reduce the number of classes from 100 to only a few, and the resulting summarized report is far more meaningful.

Formatting variables into classes

If you decide that you need to reduce the number of classes for a class variable, the simplest method for doing so is to create a temporary format that groups values. For example, if your data set has a variable called INCOME, you might want to create a format that groups the values of INCOME into $10,000 ranges. To do this, use PROC FORMAT to create a temporary format and then include a FORMAT statement in the PROC TABULATE step.† The following example illustrates this technique:

```
PROC FORMAT;
    VALUE INCFMT       .='INCOME UNKNOWN'
                  0-9999='UNDER 10,000'
              10000-19999='10,000 - 19,999'
              20000-29999='20,000 - 29,999'
              30000-39999='30,000 - 39,999'
                   OTHER='40,000 AND OVER';
PROC TABULATE FORMAT=8. MISSING;
    CLASS INCOME;
    FORMAT INCOME INCFMT.;
    TABLE INCOME;
RUN;
```

The headings produced by this example, shown in **Figure 3.5**, illustrate the six income ranges established by PROC FORMAT.

```
-------------------------------------------------------------
|                          INCOME                           |
|-----------------------------------------------------------|
| INCOME  | UNDER  |10,000 -|20,000 -|30,000 -| 40,000  |
| UNKNOWN | 10,000 | 19,999 | 29,999 | 39,999 |AND OVER|
|---------+--------+--------+--------+--------+--------|
|    N    |   N    |   N    |   N    |   N    |   N    |
|---------+--------+--------+--------+--------+--------|
```

Figure 3.5 Formatting Class Variables

---

† Refer to "The FORMAT Procedure" in the *SAS User's Guide: Basics, Version 5 Edition* or *SAS Procedures Guide for Personal Computers, Version 6 Edition* for more information on PROC FORMAT.

Note that in this figure, a separate group is created for missing values (labeled INCOME UNKNOWN). Refer to **Figure 3.4** for an illustration of what happens if missing values are not explicitly formatted.

Focusing on subgroups of classes

Occasionally you may want to analyze some observations in the input data set differently than the rest. You may need to focus on observations with values in a specific range. For example, consider a data set with income and age information. To focus on the income levels for people in the age range of 25 to 34, use PROC FORMAT to set up detailed classes for the ages you want to focus on and a general class for all other ages. The following code illustrates this technique:

```
PROC FORMAT;
    VALUE AGE25FMT  25='25'
                    26='26'
                    27='27'
                    28='28'
                    29='29'
                    30='30'
                    31='31'
                    32='32'
                    33='33'
                    34='34'
                 OTHER='ALL OTHERS';
PROC TABULATE;
    CLASS AGE;
    VAR INCOME;
    FORMAT AGE AGE25FMT.;
    TABLE AGE,INCOME*MEAN;
RUN;
```

The headings produced by this code are illustrated in **Figure 3.6**.

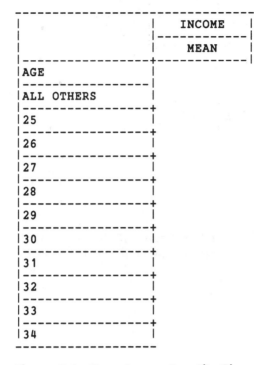

```
----------------------------------
|                   |  INCOME  |
|                   |------------|
|                   |  MEAN    |
|-------------------+------------|
|AGE                |
|-------------------|
|ALL OTHERS         |
|-------------------+
| 25                |
|-------------------+
| 26                |
|-------------------+
| 27                |
|-------------------+
| 28                |
|-------------------+
| 29                |
|-------------------+
| 30                |
|-------------------+
| 31                |
|-------------------+
| 32                |
|-------------------+
| 33                |
|-------------------+
| 34                |
----------------------------------
```

Figure 3.6 Focusing on Specific Classes

Analysis Variables

The term analysis variable is used in the context of PROC TABULATE to mean any numeric variable for which you want to compute statistics. An analysis variable is often a quantitative or continuous variable, but it can also be a qualitative or discrete variable for which you want descriptive statistics.†

The same variable can often be used as either a class variable or an analysis variable, depending upon what you need to analyze. For example, the following DATA step creates a data set with two variables: AGE and WEIGHT. The first PROC TABULATE step uses WEIGHT as the analysis variable and determines the average weight for each AGE value. The second PROC TABULATE step treats AGE as an analysis variable and calculates the average age for each WEIGHT value.

```
DATA DETAILS;
   INPUT AGE WEIGHT;
   CARDS;
1  18
2  23
3  28
4  28
1  23
2  18
3  23
4  28
1  25
1  18
```

---

† Refer to **Class or Analysis—Does It Make a Difference?** in Appendix 2 for more information on making this decision.

```
3 25
2 25
;
PROC TABULATE DATA=DETAILS;
    CLASS AGE;
    VAR WEIGHT;
    TABLE AGE,WEIGHT=' '*MEAN='AVERAGE WEIGHT';

PROC TABULATE DATA=DETAILS;
    VAR AGE;
    CLASS WEIGHT;
    TABLE WEIGHT,AGE=' '*MEAN='AVERAGE AGE';
RUN;
```

The output produced by this code is illustrated in **Figure 3.7**. Note that both TABLE statements assign a label to the heading for the analysis variable to make the heading more descriptive.

```
-------------------------------------
|                 |      AVERAGE     |
|                 |      WEIGHT      |
|-----------------+-----------------|
|AGE              |                  |
|-----------------|                  |
|1                |            21.00|
|-----------------+-----------------|
|2                |            22.00|
|-----------------+-----------------|
|3                |            25.33|
|-----------------+-----------------|
|4                |            28.00|
-------------------------------------
```

```
-------------------------------------
|                 |AVERAGE AGE      |
|-----------------+-----------------|
|WEIGHT           |                  |
|-----------------|                  |
|18               |             1.33|
|-----------------+-----------------|
|23               |             2.00|
|-----------------+-----------------|
|25               |             2.00|
|-----------------+-----------------|
|28               |             3.67|
-------------------------------------
```

Figure 3.7   Choosing How to Use a Variable: Class or Analysis

Processing Observations

Before beginning to read observations, PROC TABULATE evaluates the TABLE statement to determine what information it needs to gather. For example, this code

```
PROC TABULATE;
    CLASS DIVISION TEAM;
    VAR POINTS;
    TABLE DIVISION*TEAM*(N POINTS);
RUN;
```

requires that TABULATE find the frequency of the observations that fall into the categories created by crossing DIVISION and TEAM and the sum of the POINTS for each of these categories.

As observations are read from the data set, TABULATE creates categories from different combinations of class variable values and tallies the frequencies and sums for each category. For each observation that contains a combination of values not previously encountered, TABULATE creates a new category. For example, if the TABULATE step illustrated above processes this data set

DIVISION	TEAM	POINTS
1	2	14
1	2	27
1	1	35
2	1	63
1	2	82
2	1	45
2	1	29
1	1	85

it creates these categories and tallies these frequencies and sums:

Category	Frequency	Sum of POINTS
Division=1 ɩeam=1	2	120
Division=1 Team=2	3	123
Division=2 Team=1	3	137

This technique of summarizing information without storing observations permits TABULATE to process very large data sets in a limited amount of space. If TABULATE is processing a very large data set and runs out of memory as it is creating categories, it writes the categories, frequencies, and sums it has gathered at that point to a utility data set and begins building categories again with the remaining observations. All of these collections of categories are merged before the final output table is produced. Refer to **ESTIMATING RESOURCES** for more information.

SORTING DATA

As PROC TABULATE processes input data sets, it does not actually sort the data set. As described in **Processing Observations**, TABULATE reads observations as they occur in the data set and gathers the information needed to create the output table. As TABULATE builds categories from the input data set, they are stored by ascending sequence of the values that represent the category. (Refer to **Modifying the Order of Class Variable Values** for information on how to change the order of categories.) Thus, the output from TABULATE appears to result from a sorted data set, but sorting is not necessary for most applications and simply wastes resources.

The one time when you must sort a data set before using PROC TABULATE is when you include a BY statement in the TABULATE step. But, like sorting, BY statements are often unnecessary to produce the desired results. Refer to **Comparison of BY-Group Processing to Using the Page Dimension** for more information on BY-group processing.

Modifying the Order of Class Variable Values

By default, TABULATE orders the pages, rows, and columns of the output table in ascending order of the values of the class variables. If the categories for a class variable consist of ranges or groups of values, TABULATE uses the lowest value in the category to determine the ordering for the class. That is, if a class variable has the values illustrated in the first column below assigned to the format in the second column, the value used to store the information about the class is represented by the third column.

Actual Value	Formatted Value	Internal Identifier
1-5	PRIMARY	1
6-9,0	SECONDARY	0

Remember that by default, TABULATE does not consider the order of the formatted value, only the actual values that represent the formatted value. Thus, the order in which these values are printed is SECONDARY PRIMARY because the SECONDARY formatted value contains a lower data value than any value in PRIMARY.

You can, however, modify how TABULATE arranges the values of class variables by using the ORDER= option in the PROC TABULATE statement. You can choose to use the formatted value for ordering, or you can order the values by their frequency or by the order in which the values occur in the input data.

Consider the data set built by this DATA step. **Figures 3.8** through **3.12** illustrate the different tables produced from this data by varying the ORDER= option.

```
DATA ADS;
    INPUT AD1 AD2 AD3 AD4;
    CARDS;
3   4   3   3
1   2   1   1
2   3   1   3
3   2   2   4
4   1   2   4
1   1   3   1
2   4   3   1
2   2   3   1
3   3   4   2
1   4   4   2
1   3   4   2
2   2   4   2
3   1   1   3
3   1   1   3
4   2   1   3
1   3   2   4
2   4   2   4
2   4   4   2
3   3   3   1
4   4   3   1
;
RUN;
```

The example in **Figure 3.8** illustrates the default table produced for the data by this TABULATE step:

```
PROC TABULATE DATA=ADS FORMAT=5.;
   CLASS AD1 AD2 AD3 AD4;
   TABLE AD1 AD2,AD3 AD4 / RTS=15;
   LABEL AD1='BATHING SUIT'
         AD2='BUSINESS SUIT'
         AD3='COMPUTERIZED OFFICE'
         AD4='TRADITIONAL HOME';
RUN;
```

Note that the values of the class variables in the table are unformatted; the LABEL statement assigns descriptive headings to the names of the class variables.

	COMPUTERIZED OFFICE				TRADITIONAL HOME			
	1	2	3	4	1	2	3	4
	N	N	N	N	N	N	N	N
BATHING SUIT								
1	1	1	1	2	2	2	.	1
2	1	1	2	2	2	2	1	1
3	2	1	2	1	1	1	3	1
4	1	1	1	.	1	.	1	1
BUSINESS SUIT								
1	2	1	1	.	1	.	2	1
2	2	1	1	1	2	1	1	1
3	1	1	1	2	1	2	1	1
4	.	1	3	2	2	2	1	1

Figure 3.8   Default Order of Unformatted Classes

Figure 3.9 illustrates how the table appears when the class values are formatted into fewer categories. Note that in the code that produces **Figure 3.9**, the TABULATE statement has not changed. Because this example does not specify the ORDER= option in the TABULATE statement, the headings are ordered by the lowest internal value for each class (1 and 3 for these classes) and not the formatted values (DISLIKE and LIKE). This ordering is the default and is the same as specifying the ORDER=INTERNAL option.

```
PROC FORMAT;
   VALUE RESPONSE 3-4='DISLIKE'
                  1-2='LIKE';
PROC TABULATE DATA=ADS FORMAT=10.;
   CLASS AD1 AD2 AD3 AD4;
   FORMAT AD1 AD2 AD3 AD4 RESPONSE.;
   TABLE AD1 AD2,AD3 AD4 / RTS=15;
```

```
            LABEL AD1='BATHING SUIT'
                  AD2='BUSINESS SUIT'
                  AD3='COMPUTERIZED OFFICE'
                  AD4='TRADITIONAL HOME';
         RUN;
```

Thus, in **Figure 3.9**, LIKE (values 1 and 2) appears before DISLIKE (values 3 and 4) for all variables.

	COMPUTERIZED OFFICE		TRADITIONAL HOME	
	LIKE	DISLIKE	LIKE	DISLIKE
	N	N	N	N
BATHING SUIT				
LIKE	4	7	8	3
DISLIKE	5	4	3	6
BUSINESS SUIT				
LIKE	6	3	4	5
DISLIKE	3	8	7	4

Figure 3.9   Default Order of Formatted Classes

Figure 3.10 illustrates how the output in **Figure 3.9** changes when you add the ORDER=FORMATTED option to the TABULATE statement.

```
      PROC TABULATE DATA=ADS FORMAT=10. ORDER=FORMATTED;
         CLASS AD1 AD2 AD3 AD4;
         FORMAT AD1 AD2 AD3 AD4 RESPONSE.;
         TABLE AD1 AD2,AD3 AD4 / RTS=15;
         LABEL AD1='BATHING SUIT'
               AD2='BUSINESS SUIT'
               AD3='COMPUTERIZED OFFICE'
               AD4='TRADITIONAL HOME';
      RUN;
```

All four class variables are now ordered by the formatted values, DISLIKE and LIKE.

```
---------------------------------------------------------------
|             | COMPUTERIZED OFFICE | TRADITIONAL HOME   |
|             |---------------------+--------------------|
|             | DISLIKE  |   LIKE   | DISLIKE  |   LIKE  |
|             |----------+----------+----------+---------|
|             |    N     |    N     |    N     |    N    |
|-------------+----------+----------+----------+---------|
|BATHING SUIT |          |          |          |         |
|-------------|          |          |          |         |
|DISLIKE      |        4 |        5 |        6 |       3 |
|-------------+----------+----------+----------+---------|
|LIKE         |        7 |        4 |        3 |       8 |
|-------------+----------+----------+----------+---------|
|BUSINESS SUIT|          |          |          |         |
|-------------|          |          |          |         |
|DISLIKE      |        8 |        3 |        4 |       7 |
|-------------+----------+----------+----------+---------|
|LIKE         |        3 |        6 |        5 |       4 |
---------------------------------------------------------------
```

Figure 3.10   Changing the Order of Classes with ORDER=FORMATTED

The example in **Figure 3.11** shows the result of using the ORDER=DATA option. Remember that the first observation for the input data set had the values

AD1=3 AD2=4 AD3=3 AD4=3

which all translate to the formatted value DISLIKE.

The ORDER=DATA option uses the first values encountered for each class variable to determine the order of the table headings. Because the class variables in the following example have only two values, DISLIKE and LIKE, the first observation provides sufficient information for TABULATE to order the headings for the table. Thus, TABULATE orders the class variables by which values occurred first in the input data set. For all four variables, a DISLIKE value (3 or 4) occurs first.

```
PROC TABULATE DATA=ADS FORMAT=10. ORDER=DATA;
   CLASS AD1 AD2 AD3 AD4;
   FORMAT AD1 AD2 AD3 AD4 RESPONSE.;
   TABLE AD1 AD2,AD3 AD4 / RTS=15;
   LABEL AD1='BATHING SUIT'
         AD2='BUSINESS SUIT'
         AD3='COMPUTERIZED OFFICE'
         AD4='TRADITIONAL HOME';
RUN;
```

The output produced by this code is illustrated in **Figure 3.11**.

	COMPUTERIZED OFFICE		TRADITIONAL HOME	
	DISLIKE	LIKE	DISLIKE	LIKE
	N	N	N	N
BATHING SUIT				
DISLIKE	4	5	6	3
LIKE	7	4	3	8
BUSINESS SUIT				
DISLIKE	8	3	4	7
LIKE	3	6	5	4

Figure 3.11   Changing the Order of Classes with ORDER=DATA

Note that when ORDER=DATA is specified, the order is established from the order that the observations are read from the data set. The order for the values of one class variable is determined independently of other class variables and remains in effect across all categories. Consider this simple DATA step and PROC TABULATE coding:

```
DATA;
    INPUT ANIMAL $ FOOD $;
    CARDS;
CAT MILK
DOG BONE
DOG MILK
;
PROC TABULATE ORDER=DATA;
    CLASS ANIMAL FOOD;
    TABLE ANIMAL*FOOD;
RUN;
```

The headings produced for this code, illustrated in **Figure 3.12**, show that the order of the FOOD variable does not change for each category of ANIMAL; the order remains in effect for the entire data set.

ANIMAL		
CAT	DOG	
FOOD	FOOD	
MILK	MILK	BONE
N	N	N

Figure 3.12   ORDER=DATA Affects the Entire Data Set

Figure 3.13 illustrates the result of using the ORDER=FREQ option. The ORDER=FREQ option indicates that you want to order the values of the class variables so the value that occurs most frequently in the data set appears first.† Note that the values printed in the table in **Figure 3.13** show the frequency of each category. These are **not** the values used to order the output. PROC TABULATE uses the frequency of the values of class variables, not of categories.

```
PROC TABULATE DATA=ADS FORMAT=10. ORDER=FREQ;
   CLASS AD1 AD2 AD3 AD4;
   FORMAT AD1 AD2 AD3 AD4 RESPONSE.;
   TABLE AD1 AD2,AD3 AD4 / RTS=15;
   LABEL AD1='BATHING SUIT'
         AD2='BUSINESS SUIT'
         AD3='COMPUTERIZED OFFICE'
         AD4='TRADITIONAL HOME';
RUN;
```

Thus, LIKE appears first for the AD1 variable because the values 1 and 2 occurred more frequently (11 occurrences) than the values 3 and 4 (9 occurrences).

	COMPUTERIZED OFFICE		TRADITIONAL HOME	
	DISLIKE	LIKE	LIKE	DISLIKE
	N	N	N	N
BATHING SUIT				
LIKE	7	4	8	3
DISLIKE	4	5	3	6
BUSINESS SUIT				
DISLIKE	8	3	7	4
LIKE	3	6	4	5

Figure 3.13 Changing the Order of Classes with ORDER=FREQ

Comparison of BY-Group Processing to Using the Page Dimension

Because of the method TABULATE uses for gathering information by categories, most uses of BY-group processing can be replaced in a PROC TABULATE step by using the page dimension. In most cases, you use the BY statement to group data by distinct values of certain variables. That is exactly how TABULATE gathers and presents information in tables; thus, specifying a BY statement is usually unnecessary.

The major difference between using the page dimension of PROC TABULATE and using a BY statement is that BY-group processing requires considerably more resources for the system to run the job. BY-group processing requires that you sort the input data set; TABULATE does not need sorted data. In addition, when

---

† If two values of a class variable occur with the same frequency, TABULATE orders those headings in the reverse order of their occurrence in the data set; that is, the one that was encountered first is printed last.

you specify a BY statement in the PROC TABULATE step, TABULATE has to repeat for each BY group certain tasks that it normally performs only once for the data set.

In most cases, it is simply a matter of choice whether you use BY statements or the page dimension of PROC TABULATE to generate multiple page reports. In some situations, however, you must use one method in particular to achieve a specific purpose. This list summarizes when a specific method is required:

- If you are using the ORDER=DATA or the ORDER=FREQ option in the PROC TABULATE statement and you want the ordering to be initialized for each new page of the table, you must use a BY statement. If you want the same order to apply to all pages of the table, you must use the page dimension instead of a BY statement.
- If you want to calculate the percentage of the value in one cell to a total for the entire report, you must use the page dimension instead of a BY statement. (To do this, use the page dimension variables in the denominator definition.) If you want to calculate percentages using a total derived from a single page, you can choose either method: BY-group processing or the page dimension. (To do this using the page dimension, simply omit the page dimension variables from the denominator definition.)
- If you want to embed the heading for the page within the output table, you must use the page dimension and the BOX=_PAGE_ option in the TABLE statement.
- If you want all pages of the table to have uniform headings, it is better to use the page dimension and specify the PRINTMISS option. It is possible to print uniform headings with BY-group processing, but you might need to insert dummy observations into some BY groups that do not have all classes represented.
- If you have two ranges of values with the same format, PROC TABULATE produces different output for tables that use the page dimension than for BY groups. When you use this format for a variable in the page dimension,

```
PROC FORMAT;
   VALUE TEMP
   1-9  ='OUT OF RANGE'
   10-20='IN RANGE'
   21-30='OUT OF RANGE';
RUN;
```

TABULATE produces two pages: one for all values of OUT OF RANGE and one for IN RANGE. If you use this format for a variable in a BY statement, TABULATE produces three pages of output: one for each range listed.

Figure 3.14 illustrates the result of BY-group processing in the PROC SORT step and PROC TABULATE step shown below. Note how similar this output is to the output in **Figure 3.15**, which omits BY-group processing.

```
DATA SANSORT;
   LENGTH RACE $ 1 SEX $ 1 MARISTAT $ 1;
   INPUT a1 RACE $ a5 SEX $ a9 INCOME a17 MARISTAT $;
   CARDS;
B   F   10000   M
F   F   32000   M
B   F   56000   M
```

```
        F    F    77000    M
        F    F    35000    S
        B    F    19000    M
        B    F    44000    M
        B    M    27000    S
        B    M    12000    M
        F    M    43000    S
        B    M    67000    S
        F    M    84000    S
        F    M    43000    M
        B    F    22000    S
        B    F    49000    S
        ;
   PROC SORT DATA=SANSORT OUT=BYRACE;
      BY RACE;
   PROC TABULATE DATA=BYRACE;
      CLASS SEX MARISTAT;
      VAR INCOME;
      BY RACE;
      TABLE SEX,MARISTAT*INCOME*MEAN;
   RUN;
```

This code produces the output in **Figure 3.14**.

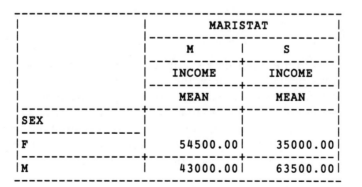

RACE=B

```
-----------------------------------------------------
|                    |          MARISTAT            |
|                    |------------------------------|
|                    |     M       |     S          |
|                    |-------------+----------------|
|                    |   INCOME    |   INCOME       |
|                    |-------------+----------------|
|                    |    MEAN     |    MEAN        |
|--------------------+-------------+----------------|
|SEX                 |             |                |
|--------------------|             |                |
|F                   |    32250.00 |    35500.00    |
|--------------------+-------------+----------------|
|M                   |    12000.00 |    47000.00    |
-----------------------------------------------------
```

RACE=W

```
-----------------------------------------------------
|                    |          MARISTAT            |
|                    |------------------------------|
|                    |     M       |     S          |
|                    |-------------+----------------|
|                    |   INCOME    |   INCOME       |
|                    |-------------+----------------|
|                    |    MEAN     |    MEAN        |
|--------------------+-------------+----------------|
|SEX                 |             |                |
|--------------------|             |                |
|F                   |    54500.00 |    35000.00    |
|--------------------+-------------+----------------|
|M                   |    43000.00 |    63500.00    |
-----------------------------------------------------
```

Figure 3.14 BY-Group Processing with PROC TABULATE

The TABULATE step below omits BY-group processing and therefore does not need the PROC SORT step. The resulting output, illustrated in **Figure 3.15**, is almost identical to that in **Figure 3.14**.

```
PROC TABULATE DATA=SANSORT;
   CLASS RACE SEX MARISTAT;
   VAR INCOME;
   TABLE RACE,SEX,MARISTAT*INCOME*MEAN;
RUN;
```

This code produces the output in **Figure 3.15**.

```
RACE  B
--------------------------------------------------------
|                     |                MARISTAT         |
|                     |---------------------------------|
|                     |      M        |       S         |
|                     |---------------+-----------------|
|                     |    INCOME     |     INCOME      |
|                     |---------------+-----------------|
|                     |     MEAN      |      MEAN       |
|---------------------+---------------+-----------------|
|SEX                  |               |                 |
|---------------------|               |                 |
|F                    |    32250.00   |     35500.00    |
|---------------------+---------------+-----------------|
|M                    |    12000.00   |     47000.00    |
--------------------------------------------------------

RACE  W
--------------------------------------------------------
|                     |                MARISTAT         |
|                     |---------------------------------|
|                     |      M        |       S         |
|                     |---------------+-----------------|
|                     |    INCOME     |     INCOME      |
|                     |---------------+-----------------|
|                     |     MEAN      |      MEAN       |
|---------------------+---------------+-----------------|
|SEX                  |               |                 |
|---------------------|               |                 |
|F                    |    54500.00   |     35000.00    |
|---------------------+---------------+-----------------|
|M                    |    43000.00   |     63500.00    |
--------------------------------------------------------
```

Figure 3.15   Replacing BY Groups with the Page Dimension

MISSING VALUES

Missing values for variables in the input data set affect the output from PROC TABULATE differently depending upon how the variables are used in the TABULATE step. Missing values for class variables cause observations to be omitted from the analysis performed to produce tables. Missing values for analysis variables affect only the statistics for those variables. A different type of missing value that is often confused with missing values in observations is the missing value used to represent empty table cells. Each of these topics is discussed in detail in this section.

How Missing Values for Class Variables Affect Output

By default, when PROC TABULATE encounters an observation that has missing values for one or more of the variables in the CLASS statement, it skips that observation. Note that TABULATE omits observations with missing class values whether the variable is used in a TABLE statement or not.

Omitting observations with missing class values can drastically affect the results you produce from a data set. In the following example, missing values in the GRADUATE variable cause a large portion of the data to be omitted from the two tables produced by this DATA and PROC TABULATE step:

```
DATA GRADS;
   INPUT RACE $ SEX $ INCOME GRADUATE $;
   CARDS;
B   F   10000   .
W   F   32000   Y
B   F   56000   Y
W   F   77000   Y
W   F   35000   .
W   F   12000   .
B   F   19000   .
B   F   44000   Y
B   M   27000   .
B   M   12000   .
B   M   36000   .
W   M   43000   Y
B   M   67000   Y
W   M   84000   Y
W   M   43000   .
B   F   22000   .
B   F   49000   Y
;
PROC TABULATE DATA=GRADS FORMAT=12.;
   CLASS RACE SEX GRADUATE;
   VAR INCOME;
   TABLE RACE*SEX ALL,GRADUATE ALL;
   TABLE RACE*SEX ALL,(GRADUATE ALL)*INCOME*MEAN*F=12.2;
RUN;
```

The first table in **Figure 3.16** illustrates the effect of a missing class variable on a table consisting of only class variables. The second table in this output shows that the results for analysis variables are also affected by missing values for class variables. Compare the values in the ALL columns of these two tables to those in **Figure 3.17** to see how the MISSING option changes the output.

You can change how TABULATE handles missing values for class variables by specifying the MISSING option in the PROC TABULATE statement. When this option is in effect, TABULATE simply treats missing values like any other value of a class variable and creates categories for all combinations of this value and the values of other variables.†

---

† Each special missing value is a distinct value for the class variable.

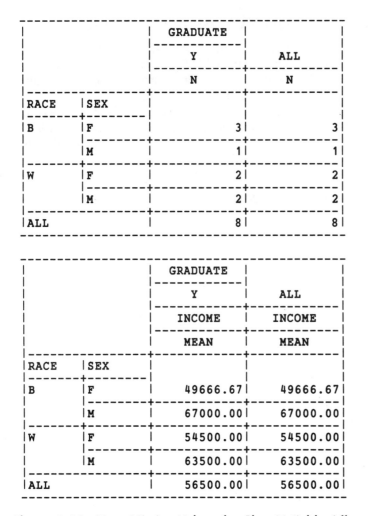

Figure 3.16 How Missing Values for Class Variable Affect Output

When the MISSING option is added to the PROC TABULATE step shown above,

```
PROC TABULATE DATA=GRADS FORMAT=12. MISSING;
   CLASS RACE SEX GRADUATE;
   VAR INCOME;
   TABLE RACE*SEX ALL,GRADUATE ALL;
   TABLE RACE*SEX ALL,(GRADUATE ALL)*INCOME*MEAN*F=12.2;
RUN;
```

the results are noticeably different for both tables, as illustrated in **Figure 3.17**. The first column for the GRADUATE variable reports the totals for observations that have missing values for GRADUATE.

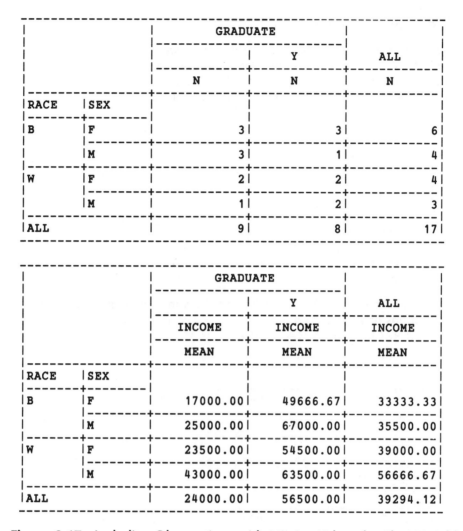

Figure 3.17 Including Observations with Missing Values for Class Variables

How Missing Values for Analysis Variables Affect Output

If the TABULATE procedure encounters an observation with a missing value for an analysis variable, it does not omit the observation as it does when the value of a class variable is missing. The missing value for an analysis variable is reflected in the counts for N and NMISS, but it is not included in the calculation for any other statistic.† The missing value does not increase the sum, and it is not counted when calculating other statistics, such as MEAN.

If all of the values for an analysis variable in a category are missing, the table cell or cells that report descriptive statistics for the variable contain missing values. That is, if all values of X are missing when A=1 and B=1 and you request this table

```
TABLE A,B*X*(MEAN STD);
```

the cells for both the MEAN and STD for the A=1 B=1 category will contain missing values.

---

† Refer to **STATISTICS AVAILABLE WITH PROC TABULATE**, in Chapter 2, for a description of NMISS.

Missing Values in Table Cells

Missing values can appear in table cells for several reasons. As described in **How Missing Values for Analysis Variables Affect Output**, missing values in table cells can indicate that the analysis variable had all missing values for that category. Missing values in table cells where two class variables intersect indicate that no observations had that combination of values.

```
DATA SIMPLE;
    INPUT SEX RACE;
    CARDS;
F    W
M    B
;
PROC TABULATE DATA=SIMPLE;
    CLASS SEX RACE;
    TABLE SEX,RACE;
RUN;
```

Figure 3.18 illustrates a table with missing values in table cells to indicate that no observations had those combinations of values. That is, no observations had SEX=M and RACE=W or SEX=F and RACE=B.

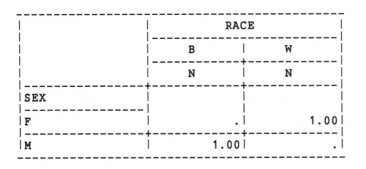

Figure 3.18   Table Cells with Missing Values

Occasionally missing values are generated for the table cells of an entire column or row, but other pages of the same report contain nonmissing values for the same column or row. By default, PROC TABULATE evaluates each page it prints and omits columns and rows for combinations of class variable values that do not exist. To change the default, you can specify the PRINTMISS option in the TABLE statement, and TABULATE will print the same headings for each subtable. Note that if an entire page of the report contains missing values, the PRINTMISS option has no effect on it; that page is not printed.

TABULATE provides a special option that allows you to modify table cells that contain missing values by replacing the standard representation, a period, with up to 20 characters of text. Use the MISSTEXT= option in the TABLE statement to define the text you want to print for missing values.

HOW PERCENTAGES ARE CALCULATED

PROC TABULATE provides the PCTN and PCTSUM statistics to allow you to print the percentage of the value in a single cell to the value in another cell or to the total of a group of cells. This section describes how TABULATE calculates percentages for the TABLE statements you specify. Refer to Chapter 4, "Learning to Use PROC TABULATE," for detailed instructions on how to request percentages in TABLE statements.

The standard method of calculating percentages is to sum a series of numbers and then divide an individual number by the sum. For example, consider the following information on school fund-raising sales:

Child	Pencils	Tablets	Total Items
Ann	4	8	12
Mary	5	10	15
John	6	4	10
Bob	2	3	5

From this information you can calculate what portion Ann's pencil sales (4) represent of her total sales (12), the total pencil sales for the girls (9), the total items sold by girls (27), or the total items sold by all the children (42). You can calculate percentages by using each of the totals above as the denominator and dividing it into 4, Ann's pencil sales.

When you want PROC TABULATE to calculate percentages, you define the total you want TABULATE to use as the denominator.† To do this, you construct the PCTN or PCTSUM expression using a denominator definition. The denominator definition describes to TABULATE what categories of information should be summed to arrive at the denominator.

The rest of this section uses this expanded version of the example above to illustrate how TABULATE sums, or collapses, categories of information to determine denominators.

```
DATA FUNDRAIS;
    INPUT @1 TEAM $ @6 GRADE @8 CLASSRM $ @10 NAME $
          @19 PENCILS @23 TABLETS;
    TOTSALE=PENCILS+TABLETS;
    CARDS;
BLUE 4 A ANN       4   8
RED  4 A MARY      5  10
BLUE 4 A JOHN      6   4
RED  4 A BOB       2   3
BLUE 4 B FRED      6   8
RED  4 B LOUISE   12   2
BLUE 4 B ANNETTE   .   9
RED  4 B HENRY     8  10
BLUE 4 C KATHY     4   7
BLUE 4 C JIM       3   9
RED  4 C STEVE    13   7
BLUE 5 A ANDREW    3   5
RED  5 A SAMUEL   12  10
BLUE 5 A LINDA     7  12
RED  5 A SARA      4   .
BLUE 5 B MARTIN    9  13
RED  5 B MATTHEW   7   6
```

† If you do not define a denominator, by default TABULATE summarizes the values in all SUM cells (for the PCTSUM denominator) or all N cells (for the PCTN denominator).

```
BLUE 5 B BETH      15  10
RED  5 B LAURA      4   3
;
RUN;
```

How PROC TABULATE Calculates PCTN Values

This PROC TABULATE step produces a table that shows how many students in each classroom participated in the project, and what percentage of the total students in a grade each classroom contributed:

```
PROC TABULATE DATA=FUNDRAIS FORMAT=6.;
   CLASS GRADE CLASSRM;
   TABLE GRADE,CLASSRM*(N PCTN<CLASSRM>) / RTS=14;
RUN;
```

By specifying CLASSRM in the denominator definition, you tell PROC TABULATE that you want to sum the frequency of all occurrences of CLASSRM, no matter what value, for each value of GRADE and then use that sum as the denominator to calculate percentages. Why for each value of GRADE? Because GRADE does **not** appear in the denominator definition. Any class variable that is not included in the denominator definition maintains distinct categories; totals are calculated for each value of these variables.

The table illustrated in **Figure 3.19** shows the frequency of each category (N) and the percentage of that category (PCTN) to the total for all CLASSRMs in each GRADE. The denominator for each percentage in the first row of this example is $4+4+3$ or 11. Thus the first PCTN value is $4 \div 11$ or 36 percent.

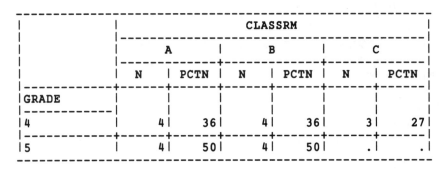

	CLASSRM					
	A		B		C	
	N	PCTN	N	PCTN	N	PCTN
GRADE						
4	4	36	4	36	3	27
5	4	50	4	50	.	.

Figure 3.19   Calculating PCTN Values for Row Totals

How PROC TABULATE Calculates PCTSUM Values

Using the data from the previous illustration, you can see the effects of denominator definitions on analysis variables. The following TABLE statement has the same denominator definition, but this time, because it is crossed with an analysis variable, it defines what values of TABLETS should be summed to calculate percentages of the SUM.

```
PROC TABULATE DATA=FUNDRAIS FORMAT=6.;
   CLASS GRADE CLASSRM;
   VAR TABLETS;
   TABLE GRADE,CLASSRM*TABLETS*(SUM PCTSUM<CLASSRM>) / RTS=14;
RUN;
```

The output from this step, illustrated in **Figure 3.20**, shows how many tablets were sold by each classroom and also compares the classroom's total to the entire grade. The denominator for each percentage in the first row of this example is 25+29+23 or 77. Thus, the first PCTSUM value is 25÷77 or 32 percent.

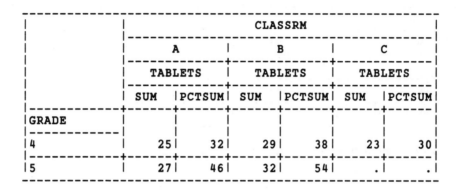

Figure 3.20   Calculating PCTSUM Values for Row Totals

Denominator Definitions in Detail

Figures 3.21 through **3.24** further illustrate how PROC TABULATE uses denominator definitions to calculate percentages. This series of figures uses the same data used to produce **Figures 3.19** and **3.20** and varies the denominator definitions to obtain various percentages. Although the examples in the rest of this section use the PCTSUM statistic to calculate percentages for analysis variables, the techniques for creating denominator definitions are the same for the PCTN statistic. The purpose of these illustrations is simply to show how to tell TABULATE which categories to sum to arrive at the denominator used for calculating percentages.

The denominator definition in this TABLE statement

```
PROC TABULATE DATA=FUNDRAIS FORMAT=6.;
   CLASS TEAM GRADE CLASSRM;
   VAR TOTSALE;
   TABLE TEAM*GRADE,
         CLASSRM*(TOTSALE*(SUM PCTSUM<TEAM*GRADE*CLASSRM>))
         / RTS=14;
RUN;
```

tells TABULATE to sum values of TOTSALE for all values of TEAM and GRADE and CLASSRM. Because all class variables are included, the denominator for the value in each SUM cell is the total of all values in the SUM of TOTSALE cells on the page. This denominator definition summarizes all of the values in the SUM cells. Omitting the denominator definition has the same effect as listing the denominator definition for all possible cells.

The value in each PCTSUM cell in the table in **Figure 3.21** is calculated by dividing the value in the SUM cell for each category by the total of all SUM cells (22+27+20+22+14+47+32+20+23+20=247). So the value of the first PCTSUM cell is 22÷247 or 9 percent.

```
---------------------------------------------------------------
|             |             CLASSRM                           |
|             |-----------------------------------------------|
|             |     A       |     B       |     C             |
|             |-------------+-------------+-------------------|
|             |   TOTSALE   |   TOTSALE   |   TOTSALE         |
|             |-------------+-------------+-------------------|
|             | SUM  |PCTSUM| SUM  |PCTSUM| SUM  |PCTSUM|
|-------------+------+------+------+------+------+------|
|TEAM  |GRADE |      |      |      |      |      |      |
|------+------|      |      |      |      |      |      |
|BLUE  |4     |  22  |   9  |  14  |   6  |  23  |   9  |
|      |------+------+------+------+------+------+------|
|      |5     |  27  |  11  |  47  |  19  |   .  |   .  |
|------+------+------+------+------+------+------+------|
|RED   |4     |  20  |   8  |  32  |  13  |  20  |   8  |
|      |------+------+------+------+------+------+------|
|      |5     |  22  |   9  |  20  |   8  |   .  |   .  |
---------------------------------------------------------------
```

Figure 3.21   Calculating Percentages of Total for Table

In the following example, the denominator definition tells TABULATE to sum values of TOTSALE for all values of TEAM and GRADE within each value of CLASSRM. That is, by omitting the CLASSRM variable from the denominator definition, you group categories by values of CLASSRM.

```
PROC TABULATE DATA=FUNDRAIS FORMAT=6.;
   CLASS TEAM GRADE CLASSRM;
   VAR TOTSALE;
   TABLE TEAM*GRADE,
         CLASSRM*(TOTSALE*(SUM PCTSUM<TEAM*GRADE>)) / RTS=14;
RUN;
```

For this denominator definition, TABULATE sets up these groups of categories and sums values of TOTSALE for each of the groups. The sum of each group is the denominator for each individual category in the group.

Group 1 CLASSRM=A	Group 2 CLASSRM=B	Group 3 CLASSRM=C
TEAM=BLUE GRADE=4	TEAM=BLUE GRADE=4	TEAM=BLUE GRADE=4
TEAM=BLUE GRADE=5	TEAM=BLUE GRADE=5	TEAM=RED GRADE=4
TEAM=RED GRADE=4	TEAM=RED GRADE=4	
TEAM=RED GRADE=5	TEAM=RED GRADE=5	

The denominator for each group is the sum of the TOTSALE for all categories in the group. Thus, the denominators are

- 22+27+20+22=91, for group 1
- 14+47+32+20=113, for group 2
- 23+20=43, for group 3.

The first PCTSUM column in the table in **Figure 3.22** is calculated by dividing the value in each cell in the SUM column by the total of SUM for group 1, 91. So the value of the first PCTSUM cell is 22÷91 or 24 percent.

```
---------------------------------------------------------------
|               |              CLASSRM                        |
|               |-----------------------------------------------|
|               |     A       |     B       |     C       |
|               |-------------+-------------+-------------|
|               |   TOTSALE   |   TOTSALE   |   TOTSALE   |
|               |-------------+-------------+-------------|
|               | SUM |PCTSUM| SUM |PCTSUM| SUM |PCTSUM|
|------------+------+------+------+------+------+------|
|TEAM |GRADE |      |      |      |      |      |      |
|-----+------|      |      |      |      |      |      |
|BLUE |4     |  22 |  24 |  14 |  12 |  23 |  53 |
|     |------+------+------+------+------+------+------|
|     |5     |  27 |  30 |  47 |  42 |   . |   . |
|-----+------+------+------+------+------+------+------|
|RED  |4     |  20 |  22 |  32 |  28 |  20 |  47 |
|     |------+------+------+------+------+------+------|
|     |5     |  22 |  24 |  20 |  18 |   . |   . |
---------------------------------------------------------------
```

Figure 3.22   Calculating Percentages of Column Totals

This TABLE statement

```
PROC TABULATE DATA=FUNDRAIS FORMAT=6.;
   CLASS TEAM GRADE CLASSRM;
   VAR TOTSALE;
   TABLE TEAM*GRADE,
         CLASSRM*(TOTSALE*(SUM PCTSUM<GRADE>)) / RTS=14;
RUN;
```

tells TABULATE to sum values of TOTSALE for all values of GRADE for each value of TEAM and CLASSRM. For this denominator definition, TABULATE sets up the following groups of categories and sums values of TOTSALE for each of the groups.

Group 1
TEAM=BLUE GRADE=4 CLASSRM=A
TEAM=BLUE GRADE=5 CLASSRM=A

Group 4
TEAM=RED GRADE=4 CLASSRM=B
TEAM=RED GRADE=5 CLASSRM=B

Group 2
TEAM=RED GRADE=4 CLASSRM=A
TEAM=RED GRADE=5 CLASSRM=A

Group 5
TEAM=BLUE GRADE=4 CLASSRM=C

Group 3
TEAM=BLUE GRADE=4 CLASSRM=B
TEAM=BLUE GRADE=5 CLASSRM=B

Group 6
TEAM=RED GRADE=4 CLASSRM=C

The denominators for each group are

- 22+27=49, for group 1
- 20+22=42, for group 2
- 14+47=61, for group 3
- 32+20=52, for group 4
- 23, for group 5
- 20, for group 6.

Thus, the values of the PCTSUM cells for the first group of categories in **Figure 3.23** are calculated by dividing each cell in the group by 49. So the value of the first PCTSUM cell is 22÷49 or 45 percent.

```
---------------------------------------------------------------
|           |              CLASSRM                            |
|           |-------------------------------------------------|
|           |      A        |      B        |      C          |
|           |---------------+---------------+-----------------|
|           |   TOTSALE     |   TOTSALE     |   TOTSALE       |
|           |---------------+---------------+-----------------|
|           | SUM  |PCTSUM| SUM  |PCTSUM| SUM  |PCTSUM|
|-----+-----+------+------+------+------+------+------|
|TEAM |GRADE|      |      |      |      |      |      |
|-----+-----|      |      |      |      |      |      |
|BLUE |4    |  22 |  45 |  14 |  23 |  23 | 100 |
|     |-----+------+------+------+------+------+------|
|     |5    |  27 |  55 |  47 |  77 |   . |   . |
|-----+-----+------+------+------+------+------+------|
|RED  |4    |  20 |  48 |  32 |  62 |  20 | 100 |
|     |-----+------+------+------+------+------+------|
|     |5    |  22 |  52 |  20 |  38 |   . |   . |
---------------------------------------------------------------
```

Figure 3.23 Calculating Percentages for a Partial Column Total

The final example in this series illustrates how to compare the value in one cell to the value in another cell. Because none of the class variables are included in the denominator definition in this TABLE statement,

```
PROC TABULATE DATA=FUNDRAIS FORMAT=4.;
   CLASS TEAM GRADE CLASSRM;
   VAR PENCILS TOTSALE;
   TABLE TEAM*GRADE,
      CLASSRM*(TOTSALE*SUM PENCILS*(SUM PCTSUM<TOTSALE>*F=6.))
      / RTS=12;
RUN;
```

TABULATE does not group any of the cells. Instead the denominator for each cell of PENCILS is the corresponding value of TOTSALE for the same category. **Figure 3.24** illustrates the output from this TABLE statement. Note that the first PCTSUM column for PENCILS is calculated by dividing 10, the SUM of PENCILS, by 22, the SUM of TOTSALE.

		CLASSRM							
		A			B			C		
		TOT-SALE	PENCILS		TOT-SALE	PENCILS		TOT-SALE	PENCILS	
		SUM	SUM	PCTSUM	SUM	SUM	PCTSUM	SUM	SUM	PCTSUM
TEAM	GRADE									
BLUE	4	22	10	45	14	6	43	23	7	30
	5	27	10	37	47	24	51	.	.	.
RED	4	20	7	35	32	20	63	20	13	65
	5	22	16	73	20	11	55	.	.	.

Figure 3.24 Calculating Percentage of One Cell in Relation to Another Cell

Calculating Percentages for Concatenated Tables

When TABLE statements have two or more expressions concatenated, or juxtaposed, in a dimension, the denominator definition becomes more complex. You must ensure that all categories crossed with the PCTN or PCTSUM statistic have a valid denominator. This usually means that you must concatenate several expressions in the denominator definition.

This situation commonly occurs when you concatenate the ALL universal class variable with one or more dimensions of the table. For example, the following code concatenates ALL in the row dimension of the TABLE statement:

```
PROC TABULATE DATA=FUNDRAIS FORMAT=6.;
   CLASS GRADE CLASSRM;
   TABLE GRADE ALL,CLASSRM*(N PCTN<GRADE ALL>) / RTS=9;
RUN;
```

The denominator definition must now define an appropriate denominator for both of these crossings:

GRADE*CLASSRM*PCTN
ALL*CLASSRM*PCTN

Because the percentages desired in this table are for column totals, the denominator definition contains all class variables in the row dimension, GRADE and ALL. The percentages produced by this code are illustrated in **Figure 3.25**.

```
|         |                      CLASSRM                                |
|         |--------------------------------------------------------------|
|         |       A        |       B        |       C        |
|         |----------------+----------------+----------------|
|         |  N   |  PCTN   |  N   |  PCTN   |  N   |  PCTN   |
|---------+------+---------+------+---------+------+---------|
|GRADE    |      |         |      |         |      |         |
|-------  |      |         |      |         |      |         |
|4        |    4 |     50  |    4 |     50  |    3 |    100  |
|---------+------+---------+------+---------+------+---------|
|5        |    4 |     50  |    4 |     50  |    . |      .  |
|---------+------+---------+------+---------+------+---------|
|ALL      |    8 |    100  |    8 |    100  |    3 |    100  |
----------------------------------------------------------------
```

Figure 3.25 Calculating Percentages for Concatenated Tables

Concatenating elements in the denominator definition can introduce some special problems. Occasionally when a denominator definition has several concatenated elements, more than one element is a valid denominator for a crossing. PROC TABULATE uses the first valid denominator definition it encounters in the TABLE statement to create the denominator for calculating percentages.

The following example illustrates how problems can occur when denominator definitions are not in the correct order. Both TABLE statements in this step define denominator definitions that summarize column totals. Both tables also include the ALL class variable in both the row and column dimensions.

```
PROC TABULATE DATA=FUNDRAIS FORMAT=4.;
   CLASS TEAM GRADE;
   VAR PENCILS TABLETS;
   TABLE ALL TEAM,
         (GRADE ALL)*(PENCILS TABLETS)*(SUM PCTSUM<TEAM ALL>)
         / RTS=8;
   TABLE ALL TEAM,
         (GRADE ALL)*(PENCILS TABLETS)*(SUM PCTSUM<ALL TEAM>)
         / RTS=8;
RUN;
```

As you can see in the first table in **Figure 3.26**, the value in the first SUM cell in each row represents the total of the SUM cells in that column, and the value in the first PCTSUM cell in each row is 100, the total of the remaining PCTSUM cells in the same column. The table produced by the first TABLE statement in the step contains the desired results.

Note the results in the second table, however. The detailed portion of the table that reports values for each grade is the same as the first table, but the PCTSUM values for the ALL columns of the second table contain incorrect values. Because the ALL element in the denominator definition is defined before the more specific element, TEAM, TABULATE used an inappropriate denominator for calculating percentages.

In general, to avoid problems with concatenated denominator definitions, specify the elements of the denominator definition from the most detailed to the least detailed. That is, put ALL or elements crossed with ALL at the end of the denominator definition. To verify that you have correctly specified the denominator definition, you should test the TABLE statement on a small set of test data.

The tables in **Figure 3.26** illustrate the effects of the different denominator definitions.

	GRADE						ALL			
	4				5				ALL		
	PENCILS		TABLETS		PENCILS		TABLETS		PENCILS		TABLETS	
	SUM	PCT-SUM	SUM	PCT-SUM	SUM	PCT-SUM	SUM	PCT-SUM	SUM	PCT-SUM	SUM	PCT-SUM
ALL	63	100	77	100	61	100	59	100	124	100	136	100
TEAM												
BLUE	23	37	45	58	34	56	40	68	57	46	85	63
RED	40	63	32	42	27	44	19	32	67	54	51	38

	GRADE						ALL			
	4				5				ALL		
	PENCILS		TABLETS		PENCILS		TABLETS		PENCILS		TABLETS	
	SUM	PCT-SUM	SUM	PCT-SUM	SUM	PCT-SUM	SUM	PCT-SUM	SUM	PCT-SUM	SUM	PCT-SUM
ALL	63	100	77	100	61	100	59	100	124	100	136	100
TEAM												
BLUE	23	37	45	58	34	56	40	68	57	100	85	100
RED	40	63	32	42	27	44	19	32	67	100	51	100

Figure 3.26 Order of Concatenated Denominator Definitions

ESTIMATING RESOURCES

The data reduction techniques described in **Processing Observations** permit PROC TABULATE to process very large data sets within limited amounts of space. You seldom need to be concerned about space requirements, but if you are processing large data sets, you may want to estimate how much additional space is required for your data.

Keep in mind that any time you run TABULATE, a certain amount of space is needed just to execute the procedure. The space required for TABULATE varies greatly depending upon your operating system and even how your site has installed the SAS System. The calculations described in this section provide information on space requirements **in addition to the basic requirements for executing PROC TABULATE and the SAS System**.

The amount of space required to process data sets is heavily dependent upon the number of variables crossed in the TABLE statement and the number of unique values of the class variables. You must have enough space available to hold a logical page of the table. That is, you must be able to store all the values in the cells that are produced by the row and column dimensions. TABULATE does not need to keep in memory all of the information generated by the page dimension of the TABLE statement.

If you must reduce the space needed to run PROC TABULATE on your data, you might want to reformat the class variables in your data set so that you have fewer classes to process. Refer to **Setting Up Useful Classes** for a discussion of how to create useful classes of variables.

In addition to storing data for each category, TABULATE also stores the characters for printing a physical page of the table. Printing requirements constitute only a small portion of the space required for very large tables, so the method for calculating this space provides only a rough estimate of the actual space used.

The following steps can help you to approximate the space requirements that vary the most:

1. Multiply the number of rows by the number of columns. When calculating the number of rows and columns, remember to include multiple iterations of each class variable or statistic that is crossed with another class variable. That is, if two class variables are crossed, A*B, you must estimate space for a complete set of B values for each value of A; if two statistics are crossed with a class variable, A*(N PCTN), you must double the space required for the values of A.
2. Multiply the result of step 1 by the size of a double precision floating-point number, which is usually 8.
3. Add to the result of step 2 the combined lengths of all formats and labels to be used in the table as column headings, row headings, and page headings.
4. Add to the result of step 3 the approximate area for printing a physical page of the table. This area will never exceed (and is often less than half) the product of multiplying the LINESIZE= value by the PAGESIZE= value.

To understand how to apply these rules, consider the TABLE statement

```
TABLE  A B, C*D;
```

which produces these crossings:

```
A*C*D
B*C*D
```

If you know the following information about the input data set, you can calculate the required space:

- The A variable has 10 distinct values; B has 30 values. Each of the variables, C and D, has 20 distinct values.
- All of the class variables are formatted, so you need to calculate space to store the character string that describes the format. The length of each format for each variable is eight characters.†
- All of the class variables have labels associated with them. As for formats, you need to add space to store the character string that describes the label. The labels for these variables are A VALUE, B VALUE, C VALUE, and D VALUE.

Using the information provided above, you can calculate the number of categories by following step 1 above. Remember that the example produces only one statistic for each category. If the example produced two statistics, you would have to double the value calculated below:

$$(10*20*20) + (30*20*20) = 16,000 \quad .$$

---

† In calculating space for them, it does not matter how labels and formats are associated with variables. You must allow space for all labels and formats, whether they are permanent or temporary.

Follow step 2 to calculate the space needed to store all categories. For the data set in the example, the calculation is as follows:

8*16000 = 128,000   .

Use this general formula to apply step 3 to the sample data set:

label length + (format length * number of formats for variable)   .

Thus, the actual space requirements for formats and labels for A, B, C, and D, respectively are

7 + (8*10) = 87
7 + (8*30) = 247
7 + (8*20) = 167
7 + (8*20) = 167   .

The combined space for labels and formats for the entire table is the sum of these four totals:

87 + 247 + 167 + 167 = 668   .

The final calculation needed is for storing a physical page. In this example, the limit on the number of printing positions required for the sample table when LINESIZE=120 and PAGESIZE=60 is

120*60 = 7200   .

Thus, for the TABLE statement illustrated here and the data set that is described above, the approximate amount of space that is required is

128000 + 668 + 7200 = 135,868   .

Remember that this 136K is only approximate and that it represents only the space needed in addition to the space for running PROC TABULATE and the SAS System.

TUTORIALS

Learning to Use PROC TABULATE

Controlling the Table's Appearance

Chapter 4

Learning to Use PROC TABULATE

An understanding of the TABLE statement is fundamental to using PROC TABULATE. This chapter explains how the TABLE statement relates to the PROC TABULATE, CLASS, and VAR statements and describes how to write TABLE statements to produce the table you want.

Recommended Use

New users: work through this chapter to learn how to use PROC TABULATE and how to construct TABLE statements.

Experienced users: refer to the chapter table of contents for topics of special interest to you.

Contents

Table

Figures

INTRODUCTION TO TABULATE STATEMENTS

In addition to the PROC TABULATE statement, which invokes the procedure, the three most important statements in the TABULATE procedure are

- the CLASS statement
- the VAR statement
- the TABLE statement.

Each of these statements is introduced in this section. The PROC TABULATE statement, the CLASS statement, and the VAR statement are used throughout the examples in this chapter to illustrate how they affect the TABLE statement. For more information on the CLASS statement and class variables, and the VAR statement and analysis variables, refer to Chapter 2, "TABULATE Procedure Description," and Chapter 3, "Details of TABULATE Processing." The TABLE statement is discussed in detail in this chapter.

PROC TABULATE Statement

The PROC TABULATE statement invokes the procedure. You can specify a number of options in this statement, but the ones most commonly used are

- DATA= identifies the input data set
- FORMAT= specifies the column width for each cell in the table.

Both of these options are used in the examples in this chapter.

CLASS Statement

The CLASS statement identifies which variables should be used to classify data into groups or categories of information. The variables listed in the CLASS statement can be character or numeric. In most cases, it is a good idea to use variables that have only a few distinct values as class variables because TABULATE prints a separate heading for each value of each class variable.

VAR Statement

The VAR statement indicates which variables should be used as analysis variables. All variables used in the VAR statement must be numeric. TABULATE calculates SUMs or other descriptive statistics for analysis variables included in the TABLE statement.

TABLE Statement

The TABLE statement describes the table that you want TABULATE to produce. Each of the variables used in the TABLE statement must be listed in either a CLASS statement or a VAR statement.

You must specify at least one TABLE statement in a PROC TABULATE step. You can use more than one TABLE statement in the same step. The rest of this chapter discusses how to create TABLE statements.

PARTS OF THE TABLE STATEMENT

You can create tables with one, two, or three dimensions by using PROC TABULATE. One-dimensional tables have only column headings; two-dimensional tables are composed of rows and columns; and three-dimensional tables divide the output into pages with rows and columns on each page. This section describes the components of the TABLE statement and explains terms used in TABULATE processing.

Pages, Rows, and Columns

As described in Chapter 2, "TABULATE Procedure Description," the TABLE statement has the format

> **TABLE**[[*page_expression*,]*row_expression*,]*column_expression*
> / *options*;

The *page_expression*, *row_expression*, and *column_expression* are constructed in the same way and are referred to collectively as dimension expressions. Dimensions of the TABLE statement are separated by commas. The variables, statistics, and other elements you use to create a dimension expression tell PROC TABULATE what data to use in the table and what information you want to see as headings for pages, rows, and columns.

If you create a TABLE statement with only one dimension, the output table will have only column headings for the information and a single row of values. This code

```
DATA VETCLNC;
    INPUT DOCTOR $ CLINIC $ ANIMAL $;
    CARDS;
WHITE    MAIN    BIRD
BROWN    SOUTH   DOG
SMITH    MAIN    DOG
JONES    SOUTH   CAT
WHITE    MAIN    DOG
BROWN    SOUTH   CAT
SMITH    MAIN    CAT
JONES    SOUTH   DOG
WHITE    MAIN    CAT
BROWN    SOUTH   BIRD
SMITH    MAIN    DOG
JONES    SOUTH   CAT
WHITE    MAIN    DOG
BROWN    SOUTH   CAT
SMITH    MAIN    BIRD
JONES    SOUTH   CAT
;
PROC TABULATE;
    CLASS ANIMAL;
    TABLE ANIMAL;
RUN;
```

produces the simple one-dimensional table illustrated in **Figure 4.1**.

```
-------------------------------------------
|                  ANIMAL                  |
|-------------------------------------------|
|    BIRD    |    CAT     |     DOG         |
|------------+------------+-----------------|
|     N      |     N      |      N          |
|------------+------------+-----------------|
|        3.00|        7.00|          6.00   |
-------------------------------------------
```

Figure 4.1   One-Dimensional Table

When you specify two dimensions, the output table has rows and columns. The following code

```
PROC TABULATE;
   CLASS DOCTOR ANIMAL;
   TABLE DOCTOR,ANIMAL;
RUN;
```

produces the simple two-dimensional table illustrated in **Figure 4.2**.

```
---------------------------------------------------------------
|              |                    ANIMAL                     |
|              |-----------------------------------------------|
|              |    BIRD    |    CAT     |     DOG             |
|              |------------+------------+---------------------|
|              |     N      |     N      |      N              |
|--------------+------------+------------+---------------------|
|DOCTOR        |            |            |                     |
|--------------|            |            |                     |
|BROWN         |       1.00 |       2.00 |          1.00       |
|--------------+------------+------------+---------------------|
|JONES         |          . |       3.00 |          1.00       |
|--------------+------------+------------+---------------------|
|SMITH         |       1.00 |       1.00 |          2.00       |
|--------------+------------+------------+---------------------|
|WHITE         |       1.00 |       1.00 |          2.00       |
---------------------------------------------------------------
```

Figure 4.2   Two-Dimensional Table

Three-dimensional tables provide column, row, and page headings and one or more pages of rows and columns of values. Using the page dimension can replace the use of BY statements in most cases and is more efficient. Refer to Chapter 3, "Details of TABULATE Processing," for more information. The following code

```
PROC TABULATE;
   CLASS DOCTOR CLINIC ANIMAL;
   TABLE CLINIC,DOCTOR,ANIMAL / CONDENSE;
RUN;
```

produces the three-dimensional table illustrated in **Figure 4.3**.

```
CLINIC MAIN
-----------------------------------------------------------
|                    |                  ANIMAL              |
|                    |--------------------------------------|
|                    |   BIRD   |   CAT    |     DOG         |
|                    |----------+----------+----------------|
|                    |    N     |    N     |      N          |
|--------------------+----------+----------+----------------|
| DOCTOR             |          |          |                 |
|--------------------|          |          |                 |
| SMITH              |    1.00  |    1.00  |      2.00        |
|--------------------+----------+----------+----------------|
| WHITE              |    1.00  |    1.00  |      2.00        |
-----------------------------------------------------------
```

```
CLINIC SOUTH
-----------------------------------------------------------
|                    |                  ANIMAL              |
|                    |--------------------------------------|
|                    |   BIRD   |   CAT    |     DOG         |
|                    |----------+----------+----------------|
|                    |    N     |    N     |      N          |
|--------------------+----------+----------+----------------|
| DOCTOR             |          |          |                 |
|--------------------|          |          |                 |
| BROWN              |    1.00  |    2.00  |      1.00        |
|--------------------+----------+----------+----------------|
| JONES              |      .   |    3.00  |      1.00        |
-----------------------------------------------------------
```

Figure 4.3   Three-Dimensional Table

Creating an Expression

You compose expressions that define the page, row, and column dimensions of the table by combining elements and operators. Elements are the variables, statistics, and other parts of the statement that TABULATE acts on to produce the table. Operators are the symbols that tell TABULATE what actions to perform on the elements.

The elements that can be used in a dimension expression are

- class variables, which must be defined in the CLASS statement. Refer to **Class Variables** in Chapter 3, "Details of TABULATE Processing," for a full discussion of class variables.
- the universal class ALL. The ALL class is discussed in **Summarizing Categories with ALL**.
- analysis variables, which must be defined in the VAR statement. Refer to **Analysis Variables** in "Details of TABULATE Processing" for a full discussion of analysis variables.
- statistics. The available statistics are described in Chapter 2, "TABULATE Procedure Description."
- format modifiers and label assignments. Refer to Chapter 5, "Controlling the Table's Appearance," for information on format modifiers and label assignments.
- expressions formed by combining any of these elements.

You can combine these elements in the TABLE statement by using operators to indicate relationships between elements. The primary operators and the effects they produce are listed in **Table 4.1**.†

---

† There are two additional operators that are discussed in detail elsewhere in this guide. Refer to Chapter 5, "Controlling the Table's Appearance," for information on the equal sign (=). Refer to **CALCULATING PERCENTAGES** for information on how to use brackets (< >).

Table 4.1   Operators in the TABLE Statement

Operator	Action	Sample Use
Comma ,	Separates dimensions of table and crosses elements across dimensions	PAGEVAR,COLVAR,ROWVAR
Asterisk *	Crosses elements within a dimension	ELEMENT1*ELEMENT2
Blank space	Concatenates elements in a dimension	ELEMENT1 ELEMENT2
Parentheses ()	Group elements and associate operator with entire group	ELEMENT1*(MEAN SUM)

These operators are discussed in detail in this chapter.

Crossing Variables and Expressions

In this book and other discussions of PROC TABULATE, the term crossing means to combine the effects of two or more table elements. The result of combining elements depends upon what type of elements are crossed. Crossings fall into these general categories:

- class variables crossed with other class variables
- class variables crossed with an analysis variable
- any variable crossed with a statistic
- variables crossed with format modifiers.

Format modifiers are discussed in detail in Chapter 5. The other crossings are described in this section. Note that you **cannot** cross two statistics or two analysis variables. This means that all analysis variables must occur in one dimension, and all statistics must occur in one dimension. Statistics and analysis variables, however, do not have to be in the same dimension.

Important: PROC TABULATE crosses variables when you use either of two operators: the asterisk (*) or the comma (,). The crossing operator (*) tells TABULATE to nest values for one variable within the values for the other variable in the same dimension. The comma tells TABULATE to cross variables and place headings in separate dimensions of the table. The following discussion illustrates each of these crossings.

Creating tables from class variables

The values of a class variable define categories.† When you cross two class variables, the combinations of values for those variables define other categories for reporting information. TABULATE creates a separate category for each unique combination of values of class variables. That is, if you cross A with B, TABULATE provides detailed information on all the values of B for each value of A. This kind of information can be simply presented in a two-dimensional table. For example, **Figure 4.4** illustrates a table you might prepare by hand to describe employees and departments. For each department, the table gives detailed information on

---

† Refer to **How TABULATE creates categories** in Chapter 3, "Details of TABULATE Processing," for a detailed discussion of categories.

the men and women in the department. At the same time, for each sex group, the table details the departments where they work.

```
                      Employees
         Departments   Women   Men

         -----------   -----   ---
         Accounting      5      4
         Human Resources 3      2
```

Figure 4.4   Sketched Table of Men and Women in Departments

The table illustrated here is actually crossing the values of Employees (Women and Men) with the values of Departments (Accounting and Human Resources) and reporting the frequency of the observations that fall into the categories created by the crossing. You can use PROC TABULATE to present the same information. The table in **Figure 4.5** shows how TABULATE produces the same table as **Figure 4.4** when you specify the two class variables, EMPSEX and DEPT, in two dimensions.

```
DATA EMPS;
   INPUT DEPT $ EMPSEX $ LEVEL $ SALARY;
   CARDS;
ACCT M JR 18498
ACCT M JR 18498
ACCT M SR 27592
ACCT M JR 20568
ACCT F SR 27587
ACCT F SR 23646
ACCT F SR 28458
ACCT F JR 19689
ACCT F JR 20446
HR   M SR 25678
HR   M SR 23857
HR   F JR 19679
HR   F JR 21564
HR   F SR 25564
;
PROC TABULATE DATA=EMPS FORMAT=8.;
   CLASS DEPT EMPSEX;
   TABLE DEPT,EMPSEX;
RUN;
```

This coding produces the table in **Figure 4.5**.

```
-------------------------------------
|                |      EMPSEX       |
|                |-------------------|
|                |    F    |    M    |
|                |---------+---------|
|                |    N    |    N    |
|----------------+---------+---------|
|DEPT            |         |         |
|----------------|         |         |
|ACCT            |       5 |       4 |
|----------------+---------+---------|
|HR              |       3 |       2 |
-------------------------------------
```

Figure 4.5   TABULATE Table of Men and Women in Departments

In addition to using two-dimensional tables to present crossed variables, you can nest the headings in one dimension as in **Figure 4.6**. Note that the same detailed information is presented but in a different format.

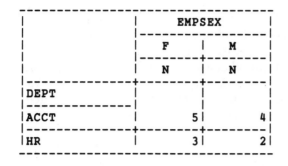

```
                    Departments
                    -----------

           Accounting              Human Resources
           Employees                  Employees
           ----------              ---------------

          Women   Men              Women   Men
          -----   ---              -----   ---
            5      4                 3      2
```

Figure 4.6   Sketched One-Dimensional Table of Employees in Departments

The nested version illustrated in **Figure 4.6** can be produced by TABULATE with the following TABLE statement:

```
TABLE DEPT*EMPSEX;
```

The table produced by this statement is illustrated in **Figure 4.7**.

```
-------------------------------------------------
|                    DEPT                       |
|-----------------------------------------------|
|        ACCT         |         HR              |
|---------------------+-------------------------|
|       EMPSEX        |       EMPSEX            |
|---------------------+-------------------------|
|    F    |    M      |    F    |    M          |
|---------+-----------+---------+---------------|
|    N    |    N      |    N    |    N          |
|---------+-----------+---------+---------------|
|       5 |        4  |       3 |        2      |
-------------------------------------------------
```

Figure 4.7   TABULATE One-Dimensional Table of Men and Women in Departments

Creating tables from analysis variables

If you specify a TABLE statement that contains only analysis variables, TABULATE summarizes all observations in the data set to produce the values in the cells of the table. Remember that you must put all analysis variables in one dimension and all statistics in one dimension, but you do not have to put the analysis variables in the same dimension as the statistics. For example, you can produce a one- or two-dimensional table when you cross SALARY with MEAN.

```
PROC TABULATE DATA=EMPS FORMAT=8.;
   VAR SALARY;
   TABLE SALARY*MEAN;
   TABLE SALARY,MEAN;
RUN;
```

The tables produced by this code are illustrated in **Figure 4.8**.

```
----------
| SALARY |
|--------|
|  MEAN  |
|--------|
|  22,952|
----------


-----------------------------
|              |   MEAN   |
|--------------+--------|
|SALARY        |   22,952|
-----------------------------
```

Figure 4.8   Simple Tables with One Analysis Variable

Crossing class and analysis variables

When you cross class variables with an analysis variable, TABULATE calculates the table cells from the values of the analysis variable for each of the categories set up by the class variables. By default, TABULATE sums the values of analysis variables within a category. For example, you might want to know the total salaries for men and women in each department illustrated in **Figure 4.7**. To produce this information, you must cross the two class variables, DEPT and EMPSEX, with the analysis variable, SALARY. You can arrange these three variables in any order and use either of the crossing operators (, or *) to produce the desired information. The coding below illustrates two of the possible methods for printing total salaries for men and women in each department:

```
PROC TABULATE DATA=EMPS;
   VAR SALARY;
   CLASS DEPT EMPSEX;
   TABLE DEPT,EMPSEX*SALARY;
   TABLE DEPT*EMPSEX*SALARY;
RUN;
```

The two tables produced by this code are illustrated in **Figure 4.9**. The first table puts the two class variables in different dimensions. The second table nests the two class variables and the analysis variable in the column dimension.

```
-----------------------------------------------------
|                   |          EMPSEX               |
|                   |-------------------------------|
|                   |      F       |      M         |
|                   |-------------------------------|
|                   |   SALARY     |   SALARY       |
|                   |-------------------------------|
|                   |    SUM       |    SUM         |
|-------------------+--------------+----------------|
|DEPT               |              |                |
|-----------------  |              |                |
|ACCT               |   119826.00  |    85156.00    |
|-------------------+--------------+----------------|
|HR                 |    66807.00  |    49535.00    |
-----------------------------------------------------
```

```
-----------------------------------------------------------------
|                              DEPT                             |
|---------------------------------------------------------------|
|           ACCT              |              HR                 |
|-----------------------------+---------------------------------|
|          EMPSEX             |            EMPSEX               |
|-----------------------------+---------------------------------|
|     F       |      M        |      F       |      M           |
|-------------+---------------+--------------+------------------|
|   SALARY    |    SALARY     |    SALARY    |    SALARY        |
|-------------+---------------+--------------+------------------|
|    SUM      |     SUM       |     SUM      |     SUM          |
|-------------+---------------+--------------+------------------|
|   119826.00 |    85156.00   |    66807.00  |     49535.00     |
-----------------------------------------------------------------
```

Figure 4.9   Crossed Class and Analysis Variables

Crossing variables and statistics

Crossing a variable (analysis or class) with a statistic tells TABULATE what type of calculations to perform. If the crossing contains no analysis variables, you can cross the class variables with only the N or PCTN statistic. By default, any time you cross class variables and do not include an analysis variable or a statistic, TABULATE automatically crosses the N statistic with the class variables. That is, this code:

```
CLASS A B;
TABLE A*B;
```

is treated like this code:

```
CLASS A B;
TABLE A*B*N;
```

Analysis variables can be crossed with any of the available statistics. If you do not specify a statistic when you include an analysis variable in the crossing, TABULATE automatically crosses the analysis variable with SUM.

The tables illustrated in **Figure 4.10** are produced by crossing an analysis variable, SALARY, with the class variables DEPT and EMPSEX and a statistic, MEAN. Both of these tables cross the same elements, but the statistic appears in different dimensions of the table.

```
PROC TABULATE DATA=EMPS FORMAT=COMMA8.;
   VAR SALARY;
   CLASS DEPT EMPSEX;
   TABLE DEPT,SALARY*EMPSEX*MEAN;
   TABLE DEPT*MEAN,SALARY*EMPSEX;
RUN;
```

The two tables produced by this code are illustrated in **Figure 4.10**. Note that you can arrange the variables in the TABLE statement in many orders. In these TABLE statements, the statistic MEAN is closest to a class variable, but it is still in the crossing with the analysis variable SALARY. Any time a statistic is included in a crossing with an analysis variable, the calculations are performed on the analysis variable. Where you place the analysis variables and the statistics in the TABLE statement affects where they appear in the headings, but it does not change the calculations.

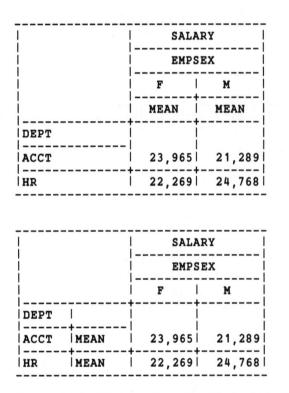

Figure 4.10   Statistic Crossed with Analysis Variable

In both of the tables in **Figure 4.10**, the first table cell contains the average salary for the women in the accounting department. TABULATE has summed the value of SALARY for the first category (EMPSEX=F, DEPT=ACCT) and calculated the mean salary.

Concatenating Variables and Expressions

Many times you find that you want to print several related variables in the same table, but it is not appropriate to cross the variables. For example, consider the employee example discussed previously. Perhaps you want to know the number of men and women in each department and the total salaries for the department, but you do not want to show the total salaries by sex. In this case, you do not want to cross EMPSEX and SALARY. You could write these two TABLE statements:

```
PROC TABULATE DATA=EMPS FORMAT=COMMA8.;
   VAR SALARY;
   CLASS DEPT EMPSEX;
   TABLE DEPT,EMPSEX;
   TABLE DEPT,SALARY;
RUN;
```

which produce the tables in **Figure 4.11**.

```
-------------------------------------------
|              |         EMPSEX            |
|              |---------------------------|
|              |    F      |      M        |
|              |-----------+---------------|
|              |    N      |      N        |
|--------------+-----------+---------------|
|DEPT          |           |               |
|--------------|           |               |
|ACCT          |        5  |          4    |
|--------------+-----------+---------------|
|HR            |        3  |          2    |
-------------------------------------------
```

```
-----------------------------
|              | SALARY      |
|              |-------------|
|              |  SUM        |
|--------------+-------------|
|DEPT          |             |
|--------------|             |
|ACCT          |  204,982    |
|--------------+-------------|
|HR            |  116,342    |
-----------------------------
```

Figure 4.11 Separate Tables from Two TABLE Statements

Or you could concatenate or juxtapose the information into one table that prints the same data under one set of headings. When you code this TABLE statement:

```
TABLE DEPT,EMPSEX SALARY;
```

TABULATE first crosses DEPT with EMPSEX and then crosses DEPT with SALARY. The resulting tables are printed side by side, as shown in **Figure 4.12**.

```
-------------------------------------------------------
|              |         EMPSEX        |               |
|              |-----------------------|               |
|              |    F     |    M       |   SALARY      |
|              |----------+------------+---------------|
|              |    N     |    N       |    SUM        |
|--------------+----------+------------+---------------|
|DEPT          |          |            |               |
|--------------|          |            |               |
|ACCT          |       5  |        4   |    204,982    |
|--------------+----------+------------+---------------|
|HR            |       3  |        2   |    116,342    |
-------------------------------------------------------
```

Figure 4.12 Tables Concatenated in the Column Dimension

Tables can also be concatenated in the row and page dimensions. The following TABULATE statements illustrate row concatenations of tables:

```
PROC TABULATE DATA=EMPS FORMAT=COMMA8.;
   VAR SALARY;
   CLASS DEPT EMPSEX;
   TABLE EMPSEX SALARY,DEPT;
RUN;
```

```
----------------------------------------
|              |           DEPT         |
|              |------------------------|
|              |   ACCT   |     HR      |
|--------------+----------+-------------|
|EMPSEX|       |          |             |
|------+-------|          |             |
|F     |N      |        5 |           3 |
|------+-------+----------+-------------|
|M     |N      |        4 |           2 |
|------+-------+----------+-------------|
|SALARY|SUM    |  204,982 |    116,342  |
----------------------------------------
```

Figure 4.13   Table Concatenated in the Row Dimension

Operations on Groups of Variables

As you write TABLE statements, you may find that you are crossing the same variable repeatedly with other variables. For example, if you want to print the number of men and women in each department and the average salary for all people in each department, you could code this TABLE statement:

```
PROC TABULATE DATA=EMPS FORMAT=COMMA8.;
   VAR SALARY;
   CLASS DEPT EMPSEX;
   TABLE DEPT*EMPSEX  DEPT*SALARY*MEAN;
RUN;
```

which produces the table in **Figure 4.14**.

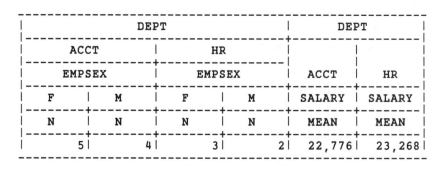

Figure 4.14   Concatenation without Grouping

But you can shorten the TABLE statement coding by using the grouping operator ( ). The TABLE statement above can be rewritten as

```
TABLE DEPT*(EMPSEX  SALARY*MEAN);
```

The grouping operator causes the operator that comes immediately before the opening parenthesis to be applied to each concatenated element inside the parentheses. This abbreviated TABLE statement produces the table in **Figure 4.15**.

```
-----------------------------------------------------------------
|                            DEPT                               |
|---------------------------------------------------------------|
|          ACCT             |             HR                    |
|---------------------------|-----------------------------------|
|   EMPSEX        |         |        EMPSEX       |             |
|-----------------|         |   |-----------------|             |
|  F   |   M   | SALARY |  F   |   M   | SALARY |
|------+-------+--------+--------+-------+--------|
|  N   |   N   | MEAN   |  N   |   N   | MEAN   |
|------+-------+--------+--------+-------+--------|
|    5 |     4 | 22,776 |     3 |     2 | 23,268 |
-----------------------------------------------------------------
```

Figure 4.15   Grouped Concatenations

In addition to grouping elements so that a single operator affects a group of elements, the parentheses also establish the order for performing operations. For example, the following TABLE statement

```
TABLE (QTR*(MON ALL) ALL)*EXPENSE*(SUM MEAN);
```

is interpreted in a series of steps that resolves the parenthetical groups from right to left, innermost to outermost. Each of the following TABLE statements produces the same information as the TABLE statement shown above although the information appears in different orders. Looking at this series of statements reveals the order in which TABULATE resolves operations on parenthetical groups.

```
1.    TABLE (QTR*(MON ALL) ALL)*(EXPENSE*SUM EXPENSE*MEAN);


2.    TABLE (QTR*(MON ALL) ALL)*EXPENSE*SUM
            (QTR*(MON ALL) ALL)*EXPENSE*MEAN;


3.    TABLE QTR*(MON ALL)*EXPENSE*SUM
            QTR*(MON ALL)*EXPENSE*MEAN
            ALL*EXPENSE*SUM
            ALL*EXPENSE*MEAN;


4.    TABLE QTR*MON*EXPENSE*SUM
            QTR*ALL*EXPENSE*SUM
            QTR*MON*EXPENSE*MEAN
            QTR*ALL*EXPENSE*MEAN
            ALL*EXPENSE*SUM
            ALL*EXPENSE*MEAN;
```

Summarizing Categories with ALL

You frequently need summary information for groups of categories as well as detailed information on each category. For example, you may want to know the average salary for men and women and the average salary for all employees. To obtain summary information on groups of categories, include the ALL universal class variable in the TABLE statement. This section discusses how to use ALL to obtain the desired information.

Summarizing all categories in a dimension

You can specify ALL in any dimension of a TABLE statement. When you concatenate ALL with other elements in the column dimension, TABULATE prints a separate column that summarizes the observations reported in each row of the table. For example, this TABULATE step:

```
PROC TABULATE DATA=EMPS FORMAT=COMMA8.;
   CLASS DEPT EMPSEX;
   VAR SALARY;
   TABLE DEPT,ALL EMPSEX SALARY*MEAN;
RUN;
```

prints the table illustrated in **Figure 4.16**. The cells in the ALL column report how many employees are in each department.

```
-------------------------------------------------------------
|              |          |      EMPSEX      |          |
|              |          |-----------------|          |
|              |   ALL    |   F    |   M    | SALARY   |
|              |----------+--------+--------+----------|
|              |    N     |   N    |   N    |  MEAN    |
|--------------+----------+--------+--------+----------|
|DEPT          |          |        |        |          |
|--------------|          |        |        |          |
|ACCT          |        9 |      5 |      4 |  22,776  |
|--------------+----------+--------+--------+----------|
|HR            |        5 |      3 |      2 |  23,268  |
-------------------------------------------------------------
```

Figure 4.16　Using ALL in the Column Dimension

When you concatenate ALL with other elements in the row dimension, TABULATE prints a separate row that summarizes the observations reported in each column of the table. For example, this TABLE statement differs from the one above only in the placement of ALL:

```
TABLE DEPT ALL,EMPSEX SALARY*MEAN;
```

The table produced by this statement is illustrated in **Figure 4.17**. The cells in the ALL row report how many women and men are employed, regardless of the department.

```
-------------------------------------------------
|              |     EMPSEX       |         |
|              |------------------|         |
|              |   F    |    M    | SALARY  |
|              |--------+---------+---------|
|              |   N    |    N    |  MEAN   |
|--------------+--------+---------+---------|
|DEPT          |        |         |         |
|--------------|        |         |         |
|ACCT          |      5 |       4 | 22,776  |
|--------------+--------+---------+---------|
|HR            |      3 |       2 | 23,268  |
|--------------+--------+---------+---------|
|ALL           |      8 |       6 | 22,952  |
-------------------------------------------------
```

Figure 4.17   Using ALL in the Row Dimension

Summarizing some of the class variables in a dimension

You can limit the scope of ALL by enclosing it within parentheses. When ALL is part of a parenthetical group, it summarizes only the categories within that group. Compare the two tables produced by these TABULATE statements:

```
PROC TABULATE DATA=EMPS FORMAT=COMMA8.;
   CLASS DEPT EMPSEX;
   VAR SALARY;
   TABLE (DEPT ALL)*EMPSEX*SALARY*MEAN;
   TABLE DEPT*(ALL EMPSEX)*SALARY*MEAN;
RUN;
```

Both of the tables produced by this code are illustrated in **Figure 4.18**. The first TABLE statement groups DEPT and ALL and crosses both of these with EMPSEX. Thus, the columns for ALL in the first table summarize all departments but maintain separate information for each sex. The second TABLE statement groups ALL and EMPSEX. The columns for ALL in the second table summarize all employees within each department.

DEPT				ALL	
ACCT		HR			
EMPSEX		EMPSEX		EMPSEX	
F	M	F	M	F	M
SALARY	SALARY	SALARY	SALARY	SALARY	SALARY
MEAN	MEAN	MEAN	MEAN	MEAN	MEAN
23,965	21,289	22,269	24,768	23,329	22,449

DEPT					
ACCT			HR		
	EMPSEX			EMPSEX	
ALL	F	M	ALL	F	M
SALARY	SALARY	SALARY	SALARY	SALARY	SALARY
MEAN	MEAN	MEAN	MEAN	MEAN	MEAN
22,776	23,965	21,289	23,268	22,269	24,768

Figure 4.18   Effect of Placing ALL in a Parenthetical Group

Summary of Rules for Creating TABLE Statements

This section summarizes many of the rules you must keep in mind when constructing TABLE statements.

- Tables can have one, two, or three dimensions. One-dimensional tables have columns only; two-dimensional tables have rows and columns; and three-dimensional tables have pages, rows, and columns.
- Commas are used to separate the dimensions of a TABLE statement.
- Within a single dimension of the TABLE statement, blanks concatenate elements.
- Within a single dimension of the TABLE statement, an asterisk crosses elements.
- The commas used to separate dimensions also have the effect of crossing the elements in the different dimensions.
- Parentheses group elements so that a single operator can affect a group of elements. For example A*(B C) crosses A with both B and C.
- You cannot cross an analysis variable with another analysis variable.
- You cannot cross two or more statistics.
- Statistics can appear in any dimension, but all statistics must be in the same dimension.
- Analysis variables can appear in any dimension, but all analysis variables must be in the same dimension.
- Statistics and analysis variables do not have to be in the same dimension.

(continued on next page)

(continued from previous page)

- For an analysis variable that does not have a statistic explicitly stated, the default statistic is SUM.
- The default statistic for class variables is N.
- The only statistics permitted for crossed class variables are N and PCTN.
- When analysis variables and statistics are included in a crossing, the statistics are calculated for the analysis variables regardless of what dimension the statistics appear in. The only difference is how the headings are ordered.
- The ALL class variable summarizes all of the class variables within a parenthetical group. If there are no parenthetical groups, ALL summarizes all class variables in the dimension where it appears.

HOW TO CREATE THE TABLE YOU WANT

When you use PROC TABULATE to produce information in tabular format, you have in mind the kind of information you want to print and a general idea of how it should look. This section helps you construct TABLE statements that produce the tables you want.

Knowing What to Expect from TABULATE

The first step in producing the desired output from TABULATE is to know how TABULATE creates tables from the TABLE statement. You have seen a number of simple TABLE statements and the resulting tables illustrated in this chapter and other chapters of the book. To illustrate how TABULATE constructs a table from a TABLE statement, let's look at a more detailed example and work through it step by step.

For example, consider the following DATA step and PROC TABULATE step:†

```
DATA EXPENSES;
   INPUT DEPT ACCT QTR MON EXPENSE @@;
   CARDS;
1 1345 1 1 12980   1 1674 1 3 13135   3 4138 1 1 29930
1 1345 1 1 9475    1 1674 1 3 21672   3 4138 1 2 22530
1 1345 1 1 15633   1 1674 1 3 3847    3 4138 1 2 16446
1 1345 1 2 14009   1 1674 1 3 2808    3 4138 1 2 27135
1 1345 1 2 10226   1 1674 1 3 4633    3 4138 1 3 24399
1 1345 1 2 16872   2 2134 1 1 34520   3 4138 1 3 17811
1 1345 1 2 17800   2 2134 1 1 25199   3 4138 1 3 29388
1 1345 1 2 12994   2 2134 1 1 41578   3 4138 1 3 16592
1 1345 1 2 21440   2 2134 1 2 26560   3 4138 1 3 12112
1 1345 1 3 35300   2 2134 1 2 19388   3 4138 1 3 19984
1 1345 1 3 25769   2 2134 1 2 31990   3 4279 1 1 9984
1 1345 1 3 42518   2 2134 1 3 24399   3 4279 1 1 7288
1 1578 1 1 8000    2 2134 1 3 17811   3 4279 1 1 12025
1 1578 1 1 5840    2 2134 1 3 29388   3 4279 1 2 14209
1 1578 1 1 9636    2 2403 1 1 25464   3 4279 1 2 10372
1 1578 1 2 7900    2 2403 1 1 18588   3 4279 1 2 17113
```

---

† Note the use of the double trailing at sign (@@) in the INPUT statement. This symbol allows you to enter multiple observations on one line. This example has three observations on each line.

```
 1  1578  1  2  5767     2  2403  1  1  30670     3  4279  1  3  13500
 1  1578  1  2  9515     2  2403  1  2  15494     3  4279  1  3  9855
 1  1578  1  3  4500     2  2403  1  2  11310     3  4279  1  3  16260
 1  1578  1  3  3285     2  2403  1  2  18661     3  4290  1  1  10948
 1  1578  1  3  5420     2  2403  1  2  1482      3  4290  1  1  7992
 1  1674  1  1  11950    2  2403  1  2  1081      3  4290  1  1  13186
 1  1674  1  1  8723     2  2403  1  2  1783      3  4290  1  2  14539
 1  1674  1  1  14392    2  2403  1  3  10009     3  4290  1  2  10613
 1  1674  1  2  13534    2  2403  1  3  7306      3  4290  1  2  17511
 1  1674  1  2  9879     2  2403  1  3  12054     3  4290  1  3  11459
 1  1674  1  2  16300    3  4138  1  1  24850     3  4290  1  3  8365
 1  1674  1  3  17994    3  4138  1  1  18140     3  4290  1  3  13802
;
PROC TABULATE DATA=EXPENSES;
   CLASS QTR MON DEPT ACCT;
   VAR EXPENSE;
   TABLE DEPT*(ACCT ALL) ALL,
         (QTR*(MON ALL) ALL)*EXPENSE*SUM;
 RUN;
```

The table requested by this code has only two dimensions, but each dimension has several variables and several types of operations: crossing, concatenating, and grouping. The complete output from this code is illustrated in **Output 4.1**; **Figures 4.19** and **4.20** show parts of this same output in greater detail. Finally, **Output 4.2** illustrates how the same table can be formatted to improve some of the row and column headings.

TABULATE creates the headings for the row dimension, illustrated in **Figure 4.19**, from the row dimension expression:

```
DEPT*(ACCT ALL) ALL
```

The first part of the expression crosses DEPT with each of the variables ACCT and ALL. The first crossing, DEPT*ACCT, tells TABULATE to list the individual accounts for each department. The next crossing summarizes all accounts for each department, DEPT*ALL. The last part of the row expression, ALL, summarizes all accounts in all departments.

TABULATE creates headings in the same order that you request them in the TABLE statement. Headings for variables crossed in the row dimension are ordered from left to right; headings for concatenated variables are listed top to bottom. Thus, in **Figure 4.19**, the headings for the departments appear to the left, followed by the accounts to the right, and the ALL category appears below the individual accounts.

The column dimension in the example

```
(QTR*(MON ALL) ALL)*EXPENSE*SUM
```

looks somewhat imposing, but the groupings, crossings, and concatenations in this expression can be interpreted as the following requests:

1. List the sum of the expenses for each month in each quarter:

```
QTR*MON*EXPENSE*SUM
```

2. List the sum of the expenses for an entire quarter:

```
QTR*ALL*EXPENSE*SUM
```

3. List the sum of the expenses for all quarters:

```
ALL*EXPENSE*SUM
```

```
|-----------------------------------+
|DEPT            |ACCT              |
|----------------+------------------|
|1               |1345              |
|                |------------------+
|                |1578              |
|                |------------------+
|                |1674              |
|                |------------------+
|                |ALL               |
|----------------+------------------+
|2               |ACCT              |
|                |------------------|
|                |2134              |
|                |------------------+
|                |2403              |
|                |------------------+
|                |ALL               |
|----------------+------------------+
|3               |ACCT              |
|                |------------------|
|                |4138              |
|                |------------------+
|                |4279              |
|                |------------------+
|                |4290              |
|                |------------------+
|                |ALL               |
|----------------+------------------+
|ALL                                |
-------------------------------------
```

Figure 4.19   Close-up of Row Headings

Figure 4.20 shows how TABULATE resolves these requests. The headings are nested and concatenated in the same order as the requests listed above: first the detailed information for each month, then the summary for the quarter, and finally the summary for all quarters year-to-date.

```
------------------------------------------------------------------
|                        QTR                        |             |
|---------------------------------------------------|             |
|                         1                         |             |
|---------------------------------------------------|             |
|               MON                 |               |             |
|-----------------------------------|               |             |
|    1    |    2    |    3    |   ALL    |   ALL    |
|---------+---------+---------+----------+-----------|
| EXPENSE | EXPENSE | EXPENSE | EXPENSE  | EXPENSE   |
|---------+---------+---------+----------+-----------|
|   SUM   |   SUM   |   SUM   |   SUM    |   SUM     |
+---------+---------+---------+----------+-----------|
```

Figure 4.20   Close-up of Column Headings

The completed output from this example is illustrated in **Output 4.1**. The values printed in the table cells are the result of crossing the row variables with the column variables. Each table cell represents the sum of the expenses for the category created when a row and column intersect. Note that in this example, the final summary is the same as the quarterly summary simply because the data set contains only first quarter data.

Output 4.1   Expenses by Month, Quarter, and Year-to-Date

		QTR				
		1				
		MON			ALL	ALL
		1	2	3	ALL	ALL
		EXPENSE	EXPENSE	EXPENSE	EXPENSE	EXPENSE
		SUM	SUM	SUM	SUM	SUM
DEPT	ACCT					
1	1345	38088.00	93341.00	103587.00	235016.00	235016.00
	1578	23476.00	23182.00	13205.00	59863.00	59863.00
	1674	35065.00	39713.00	64089.00	138867.00	138867.00
	ALL	96629.00	156236.00	180881.00	433746.00	433746.00
2	ACCT					
	2134	101297.00	77938.00	71598.00	250833.00	250833.00
	2403	74722.00	49811.00	29369.00	153902.00	153902.00
	ALL	176019.00	127749.00	100967.00	404735.00	404735.00
3	ACCT					
	4138	72920.00	66111.00	120286.00	259317.00	259317.00
	4279	29297.00	41694.00	39615.00	110606.00	110606.00
	4290	32126.00	42663.00	33626.00	108415.00	108415.00
	ALL	134343.00	150468.00	193527.00	478338.00	478338.00
ALL		406991.00	434453.00	475375.00	1316819.00	1316819.00

The row and column headings in **Output 4.1** are identical to those illustrated in **Figures 4.19** and **4.20**. Now compare these headings to the ones in **Output 4.2**. **Output 4.2** illustrates how formatting can improve the appearance of a table and make the table more meaningful. Formatting is discussed in detail in Chapter 5, "Controlling the Table's Appearance," but it is mentioned here to make you aware of how much you can alter the tables produced by TABULATE. The table illustrated in **Output 4.2** is produced with the following code. Note that the only changes are for formatting and altering headings. The same groupings, crossings, and concatenations apply to the variables.

```
PROC FORMAT;
   VALUE QTRFMT 1='FIRST QUARTER'
                2='SECOND QUARTER'
                3='THIRD QUARTER'
                4='FOURTH QUARTER';
   VALUE MONFMT 1='JANUARY'
                2='FEBRUARY'
                3='MARCH'
                4='APRIL'
                5='MAY'
                6='JUNE'
                7='JULY'
                8='AUGUST'
```

```
                          9='SEPTEMBER'
                         10='OCTOBER'
                         11='NOVEMBER'
                         12='DECEMBER';
               VALUE DEPTFMT 1='ACCOUNTING'
                            2='HUMAN RESOURCES'
                            3='SYSTEMS';

        PROC TABULATE DATA=EXPENSES FORMAT=COMMA10.2;
           CLASS QTR MON DEPT ACCT;
           VAR EXPENSE;
           FORMAT DEPT DEPTFMT. QTR QTRFMT. MON MONFMT.;
           TABLE (DEPT=' '*(ACCT=' ' ALL='SUB-TOTAL') ALL='TOTAL'),
                 (QTR=' '*(MON='MONTHLY EXPENDITURES' ALL='QUARTERLY TOTAL')
                 ALL='YEAR TO DATE TOTAL')*EXPENSE=' '*SUM=' '
                 / BOX='DEPARTMENT        ACCOUNT NUMBER';
        RUN;
```

Output 4.2   Expenses Report with Descriptive Formats and Labels

DEPARTMENT	ACCOUNT NUMBER	FIRST QUARTER				
		MONTHLY EXPENDITURES			QUARTERLY TOTAL	YEAR TO DATE TOTAL
		JANUARY	FEBRUARY	MARCH		
ACCOUNTING	1345	38,088.00	93,341.00	103,587.00	235,016.00	235,016.00
	1578	23,476.00	23,182.00	13,205.00	59,863.00	59,863.00
	1674	35,065.00	39,713.00	64,089.00	138,867.00	138,867.00
	SUB-TOTAL	96,629.00	156,236.00	180,881.00	433,746.00	433,746.00
HUMAN RESOURCES	2134	101,297.00	77,938.00	71,598.00	250,833.00	250,833.00
	2403	74,722.00	49,811.00	29,369.00	153,902.00	153,902.00
	SUB-TOTAL	176,019.00	127,749.00	100,967.00	404,735.00	404,735.00
SYSTEMS	4138	72,920.00	66,111.00	120,286.00	259,317.00	259,317.00
	4279	29,297.00	41,694.00	39,615.00	110,606.00	110,606.00
	4290	32,126.00	42,663.00	33,626.00	108,415.00	108,415.00
	SUB-TOTAL	134,343.00	150,468.00	193,527.00	478,338.00	478,338.00
TOTAL		406,991.00	434,453.00	475,375.00	1316819.00	1316819.00

Writing the Right TABLE Statement

When you know how TABULATE produces tables from TABLE statements, you will be able to write TABLE statements that produce exactly the table you have in mind. When you start to write a PROC TABULATE step, you know what information you want to produce and you probably also have a general idea of how the table should be structured. For example, let's assume your table has to provide these quarterly expenses:

• the average and total expenses for each account in each department for an entire quarter

- the average expense and a subtotal of expenses for all accounts in each department for the quarter
- the average expense and the total expenses for all accounts in all departments for the quarter.

This information can be conveyed in a number of ways, but assume that **Figure 4.21** illustrates a rough draft of the table you have in mind.

```
Quarter  Dept.  Acct.                    Expenses
-------  ----   ----    -------------------------------------
   1       1     A      total quarterly      avg. quarterly
                        expense for acct.    expense for acct.

                 B      total quarterly      avg. quarterly
                        expense for acct.    expense for acct.

         Total          total quarterly      avg. quarterly
                        expense for dept.    expense for dept.


           2     A            .                    .
                             .                    .

                 B            .                    .
                             .                    .

         Total               .                    .



   Total                total quarterly      avg. quarterly
                        expenses for all     expenses for all
                        accounts in all      accounts in all
                        depts.               depts.
```

Figure 4.21   Sketch of Needed Report

To begin developing the correct TABLE statement, start with the headings for the row dimension. You know that you want to set up headings for three class variables, QTR, DEPT, and ACCT, and you want these variables to appear in this order. You also want to nest information about accounts within each department and then nest departments within the quarter. To nest these values in the same dimension you must use the crossing operator (*). Thus, a basic part of the row dimension will be the relationship among these variables, which can be expressed as

```
QTR*DEPT*ACCT
```

In addition to the detailed information, you also need to produce department and quarterly totals. These totals can be requested by using the universal class variable, ALL. As discussed in **Summarizing Categories with ALL**, ALL summarizes information for the class variables within the same parenthetical group. If it is not contained within a group, ALL summarizes all class variables in the same dimension. The requirements for the table indicate that you need a summary for all accounts in each department. You need to group the ALL class variable with the ACCT variable, which will produce the quarterly total of all accounts in each department. Thus, you can add this to the row dimension you are building:

```
QTR*DEPT*(ACCT ALL)
```

The final requirement for the row dimension is to produce the department totals within each quarter. What this really means is that you need to summarize the account totals for all departments. Thus, you need to enclose ALL within the same group as the DEPT variable. The resulting expression is

```
QTR*(DEPT*(ACCT ALL) ALL)
```

In this example, the requirements for setting up the column dimension of the table are much simpler than the row dimension. The only variable needed in the column dimension of the sketched table in **Figure 4.21** is EXPENSE. Because you want to calculate totals and other statistics, you need to declare this as an analysis variable by placing it in the VAR statement. The first step in creating the column dimension is to list the variable, as shown here:

```
EXPENSE
```

If you use this expression for the entire column dimension, TABULATE assumes that the desired statistic is SUM. In order to produce both the sum and the average, you must cross both of these statistics with the analysis variable. Thus, the correct expression for the column dimension of the table is

```
EXPENSE*(SUM MEAN)
```

The complete coding needed to generate the desired output from TABULATE is illustrated below. If you want to alter the headings for the rows and columns, you can also add descriptive labels and format the class variable values. Techniques for formatting and labeling are discussed in detail in Chapter 5, "Controlling the Table's Appearance."

```
PROC TABULATE DATA=EXPENSES;
   CLASS QTR DEPT ACCT;
   VAR EXPENSE;
   TABLE QTR*(DEPT*(ACCT ALL) ALL),
         EXPENSE*(SUM MEAN);
RUN;
```

This code produces the table illustrated in **Figure 4.22**.

			EXPENSE	
			SUM	MEAN
QTR	DEPT	ACCT		
1	1	1345	235016.00	19584.67
		1578	59863.00	6651.44
		1674	138867.00	11572.25
		ALL	433746.00	13143.82
	2	ACCT		
		2134	250833.00	27870.33
		2403	153902.00	12825.17
		ALL	404735.00	19273.10
	3	ACCT		
		4138	259317.00	21609.75
		4279	110606.00	12289.56
		4290	108415.00	12046.11
		ALL	478338.00	15944.60
	ALL		1316819.00	15676.42

Figure 4.22   TABULATE Version of Needed Report

CALCULATING PERCENTAGES

In addition to requesting TABULATE to print sums, frequencies, and other descriptive statistics, you can also ask TABULATE to print the percentage that the value in one table cell represents of a total for a group of categories. You may want to compare the value in a single cell to

- the total of all cells in the table
- the total of all cells in the row containing the cell
- the total of all cells in the column containing the cell
- the total of all cells in a different row or column
- some other total derived from the table
- a total of a numeric variable in the data set.

You can derive two different percentages for each of these totals. If you want the percentage that the frequency reported in one cell represents of the total frequency, use the PCTN statistic. When you want to obtain the percentage that the sum of an analysis variable for one category represents of the total sum for a group of categories, use the PCTSUM statistic.

This section describes simple rules to follow to request the most frequently needed percentages. Refer to Chapter 3, "Details of TABULATE Processing," for an explanation of how TABULATE calculates percentages.

Simple Percentages

The simplest percentage you can request is the percentage of the value in one table cell to the sum of all table cells. Whether you use PCTN or PCTSUM depends upon what values are in the table cells. For example, let's return to the sample data used for **Figures 4.5** and **4.10** and request some additional information. Recall that the TABULATE statements to produce **Figure 4.5** were

```
PROC TABULATE DATA=EMPS FORMAT=8.;
   CLASS DEPT EMPSEX;
   TABLE DEPT,EMPSEX;
RUN;
```

This TABLE statement produces the number of male and female employees in each department. If you also want to know the percentage of male employees in one department to all employees, you can add the PCTN element to the TABLE statement.

The following TABULATE statements illustrate how to request both the frequencies produced by the first TABLE statement and the percentage of the frequency of each category to the total frequency of all categories (that is, the percentage of the value in one cell to the total for all cells).†

```
PROC TABULATE DATA=EMPS FORMAT=COMMA8.;
   CLASS DEPT EMPSEX;
   TABLE DEPT,EMPSEX*(N PCTN);
RUN;
```

The table produced by this code is illustrated in **Figure 4.23**.

```
-----------------------------------------------------------------
|                    |              EMPSEX                       |
|                    |-------------------------------------------|
|                    |        F         |         M              |
|                    |------------------+------------------------|
|                    |   N   |  PCTN    |   N   |    PCTN         |
|--------------------+-------+----------+-------+----------------|
|DEPT                |       |          |       |                |
|--------------------|       |          |       |                |
|ACCT                |     5 |      36  |     4 |       29       |
|--------------------+-------+----------+-------+----------------|
|HR                  |     3 |      21  |     2 |       14       |
-----------------------------------------------------------------
```

Figure 4.23   Percentages for Default PCTN Denominator

The sum of all frequencies printed in **Figure 4.23** is 14. As you can see in the table, the percentage of females in the accounting department (5) to the total employees (14) is 36, when rounded to the nearest integer.

To understand the PCTSUM statistic, you can return to the table shown in **Figure 4.10** and request some additional information. Perhaps you would like to know the percentage of the salaries for the women in the accounting department to all employees. You can request this information by using the PCTSUM statistic in the TABLE statement. To make it a little easier to see how TABULATE performs this calculation, this example prints the SUM of the salary for each sex as well

---

† Note that this TABLE statement requests two pieces of information for each category: the frequency (N) and the percentage (PCTN). The frequency is the default statistic when no other statistic is specified, as in **Figure 4.5**. When you do specify another statistic, such as PCTN, you must specifically request the frequency if you also want it printed.

as the MEAN salary and the percentage. The TABULATE statements used to produce **Figure 4.24** are as follows:

```
PROC TABULATE DATA=EMPS FORMAT=COMMA8.;
   CLASS DEPT EMPSEX;
   VAR SALARY;
   TABLE DEPT,EMPSEX*SALARY*(MEAN SUM PCTSUM) / RTS=8;
RUN;
```

This TABLE statement tells TABULATE to summarize all SUM values (119,826
+85,156+66,807+49,535) and calculate the percentage of each SUM to the
total for all employees.

		EMPSEX					
		F			M		
		SALARY			SALARY		
		MEAN	SUM	PCTSUM	MEAN	SUM	PCTSUM
DEPT							
ACCT		23,965	119,826	37	21,289	85,156	27
HR		22,269	66,807	21	24,768	49,535	15

Figure 4.24 Percentages for Default PCTSUM Denominator

Whether you are using the PCTN or PCTSUM statistics, be sure to follow these
rules:

- To request one of these percentages, include PCTN or PCTSUM in one
  of the dimensions of the TABLE statement.
- Like other statistics, PCTN and PCTSUM can appear in any dimension,
  but they must be in the same dimension as all other statistics.
- You cannot cross PCTN or PCTSUM with another statistic.
- To use PCTSUM, an analysis variable must appear in the crossing.

Rules for Requesting Percentages

There are times when the simple percentages provided by adding PCTN or
PCTSUM to the TABLE statement do not meet your needs. If you need to obtain
the percentage of the value in a single table cell to a subtotal of the entire table,
you need to specify a denominator definition for the percentage. The denominator definition describes what categories should be included in the subtotal for
calculating the percentage. The format for specifying a denominator definition
is to enclose it in brackets < > and append it to the PCTN or PCTSUM statistic.
A TABLE statement with a simple denominator definition looks like the following:

```
TABLE DEPT,EMPSEX*(N PCTN<DEPT>);
```

This denominator definition tells TABULATE to summarize all departments for each employee sex and then compare the value in each table cell to the total for that sex. The table produced by this code is illustrated in **Figure 4.25.**†

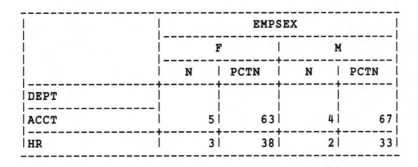

```
---------------------------------------------------
|                   |           EMPSEX             |
|                   |------------------------------|
|                   |      F       |      M        |
|                   |--------------|---------------|
|                   |  N  | PCTN   |  N  | PCTN    |
|-------------------+-----+--------+-----+---------|
|DEPT               |     |        |     |         |
|-------------------|     |        |     |         |
|ACCT               |  5  |  63    |  4  |  67     |
|-------------------+-----+--------+-----+---------|
|HR                 |  3  |  38    |  2  |  33     |
---------------------------------------------------
```

Figure 4.25   Percentages for Explicit Denominator Definition

The discussion of denominator definitions in Chapter 3, "Details of TABULATE Processing," will help you to understand how TABULATE uses a denominator definition. This section provides some simple rules for obtaining the most commonly needed percentages.

Note: it is often helpful when requesting percentages of row, column, or page totals to be able to see the total to which the value in each table cell is compared. To print this total, concatenate ALL to the dimension that is to be summarized. That is, if you want column totals, you are summarizing the data in the rows, so attach ALL to the row dimension. For example, adding ALL to the coding that produces **Figure 4.25** produces the table in **Figure 4.26**. In this table you can see the column totals to which each table cell in the column is compared.

```
TABLE DEPT ALL,EMPSEX*(N PCTN<DEPT ALL>);
```

This TABLE statement produces the table in **Figure 4.26**.

```
-----------------------------------------------------
|                   |           EMPSEX              |
|                   |-------------------------------|
|                   |      F       |      M         |
|                   |--------------|----------------|
|                   |  N  | PCTN   |  N  | PCTN     |
|-------------------+-----+--------+-----+----------|
|DEPT               |     |        |     |          |
|-------------------|     |        |     |          |
|ACCT               |  5  |  63    |  4  |  67      |
|-------------------+-----+--------+-----+----------|
|HR                 |  3  |  38    |  2  |  33      |
|-------------------+-----+--------+-----+----------|
|ALL                |  8  | 100    |  6  | 100      |
-----------------------------------------------------
```

Figure 4.26   Adding ALL to Clarify Percentage Calculations

---

† Rounding the percentage to the nearest integer may cause the total of the percentages to be not exactly 100.

Requesting the percentage of column totals

The rule to follow for requesting percentages of column totals is to build the denominator definition of all the class variables that define a single row of the table. If you have several class variables concatenated in the row dimension, you must include all of them in the denominator definition. TABULATE selects the appropriate denominator to calculate percentages.†

The table in **Figure 4.26** illustrates a simple example of obtaining the percentage of the value in a single cell to the total for the column that contains the cell. By specifying the row variable DEPT in the denominator definition, you tell TABULATE to sum all rows (all departments) for a single column (each sex) and use that total as the denominator for calculating the percentage. Including ALL in the denominator definition provides an appropriate denominator for the cell that reports all female employees.

The total for all cells in the first column is 8, so the percentage of the value in the first cell, 5, to the column total is $5 \div 8$, or 63 percent. The other cell in the same column has a frequency of 3, which is 38 percent of the column total. Because the value in the ALL table cell for females is the same as the denominator, 8, the PCTN value is 100 percent. When TABULATE calculates the percentages for the male employees, it uses the total shown in the ALL table cell for men, 6. The two PCTN values for men are $4 \div 6$, or 67 percent of the total, and $2 \div 6$, which is the remaining 33 percent.

Now let's consider how to obtain percentages for a more complex TABLE statement. Remember that to obtain percentages of column totals, you need to include in the denominator definition all of the variables that describe the rows you want to total. For example, the row dimension in the TABLE statement below crosses two class variables and concatenates them with ALL:

```
PROC TABULATE DATA=EMPS FORMAT=8.;
   CLASS DEPT EMPSEX LEVEL;
   TABLE DEPT*LEVEL ALL,EMPSEX*(N PCTN<DEPT*LEVEL ALL>);
RUN;
```

DEPT and LEVEL must be crossed in the denominator definition and concatenated with ALL to get the percentage of the value in each cell to the column total. As you can see in **Figure 4.27**, the column total for the first column is 8. Thus the value in the first cell, 2, is 25 percent of the column total.

| | | EMPSEX | | | |
| | | F | | M | |
DEPT	LEVEL	N	PCTN	N	PCTN
ACCT	JR	2	25	3	50
	SR	3	38	1	17
HR	JR	2	25	.	.
	SR	1	13	2	33
ALL		8	100	6	100

Figure 4.27   Percentages of Column Totals

---

† Refer to **Calculating Percentages for Concatenated Tables** in Chapter 3 for more information.

Requesting the percentage of row totals

The rule for requesting the percentage of row totals is to build the denominator definition of all class variables that define the columns to be summarized. The TABLE statement below illustrates the rule for obtaining the percentage of the value in one cell to the row total. These statements

```
PROC TABULATE DATA=EMPS FORMAT=COMMA6.;
   CLASS DEPT EMPSEX LEVEL;
   VAR SALARY;
   TABLE DEPT,
         LEVEL*EMPSEX*SALARY*(SUM PCTSUM<LEVEL*EMPSEX>) / RTS=7;
RUN;
```

tell TABULATE to summarize the SUM columns for each row of the table and then calculate the percentage of each SUM to the row that contains it. If you look at the table produced by this code, illustrated in **Figure 4.28**, you can see the values that TABULATE summarizes. To calculate the percentages for the accounting department, TABULATE adds the total salaries for all employees in the department, (40,135+57,564+79,691+27,592=204,982), and then calculates the percentage of the value in each SUM cell to the department total. Thus, 40,135 is 20 percent of the total.

```
------------------------------------------------------------------------
|      |                              LEVEL                             |
|      |----------------------------------------------------------------|
|      |              JR               |              SR                |
|      |-------------------------------+--------------------------------|
|      |            EMPSEX             |            EMPSEX              |
|      |-------------------------------+--------------------------------|
|      |     F       |      M          |     F        |      M          |
|      |-------------+-----------------+--------------+----------------|
|      |   SALARY    |    SALARY       |   SALARY     |    SALARY       |
|      |-------------+-----------------+--------------+----------------|
|      | SUM  |PCTSUM| SUM   |PCTSUM   | SUM   |PCTSUM| SUM   |PCTSUM  |
|------+------+------+-------+------+--------+------+-------+------|
|DEPT  |      |      |       |      |        |      |       |      |
|------|      |      |       |      |        |      |       |      |
|ACCT  |40,135|   20 |57,564 |   28 |79,691  |   39 |27,592 |   13 |
|------+------+------+-------+------+--------+------+-------+------|
|HR    |41,243|   35 |    .  |   .  |25,564  |   22 |49,535 |   43 |
------------------------------------------------------------------------
```

Figure 4.28 Percentages of Row Totals

Requesting the percentage of page totals

The rule for requesting the percentage of page totals is to cross all class variables of the row and column dimensions to form the denominator. Calculating page totals differs from requesting simple percentages (using PCTN and PCTSUM without denominators) because simple percentages summarize all pages of the table. Denominators for page totals summarize only a single page.

These TABULATE statements

```
PROC TABULATE DATA=EMPS FORMAT=COMMA7.;
   CLASS DEPT EMPSEX LEVEL;
   VAR SALARY;
   TABLE DEPT,
         LEVEL,EMPSEX*SALARY*(SUM PCTSUM<LEVEL*EMPSEX>);
RUN;
```

illustrate the rule for percentages of page totals. As you can see in **Figure 4.29**, the value in each SUM cell on the page is compared to the total of all SUM cells on the page to determine the percentage. The total for the page is $40,135+57,564+79,691+27,592=204,982$ and so 40,135 is 20 percent of the total.

DEPT ACCT

		EMPSEX			
		F		M	
		SALARY		SALARY	
		SUM	PCTSUM	SUM	PCTSUM
LEVEL					
JR		40,135	20	57,564	28
SR		79,691	39	27,592	13

DEPT HR

		EMPSEX			
		F		M	
		SALARY		SALARY	
		SUM	PCTSUM	SUM	PCTSUM
LEVEL					
JR		41,243	35	.	.
SR		25,564	22	49,535	43

Figure 4.29 Percentages of Page Totals

Requesting the percentage of other totals

You can request TABULATE to print the percentage of the value in a cell in one row or column to the total for another row or column in the table. You can request the percentage of the value in a cell to a total for a subgroup of a row or column. In fact, you can construct many denominator definitions for which there are no simple formulas. As you construct denominator definitions other than the standard ones described in this section, a thorough understanding of how TABULATE processes denominators is essential. Refer to Chapter 3, "Details of TABULATE Processing," for a more detailed discussion of denominators.

Summary of the Rules for Denominator Definitions

When constructing a denominator definition to calculate percentages, be sure to follow these rules:

- A denominator definition can contain

    a single variable
    crossings of class variables
    crossings of class variables and one analysis variable
    concatenations of any of the above.

- All class variables used in a denominator definition must appear in the TABLE statement.
- No grouping is permitted in denominator definitions. That is, you must say <A*B A*C>. You cannot use A*(B C) within brackets.
- When constructing a denominator definition, work out all crossings and be sure at least one operand in the denominator definition appears in each crossing that is affected by the denominator. In this statement

```
TABLE A ALL,C (B ALL)*(N PCTN<B ALL>);
```

the denominator definition could not be just ALL or just B; it has to be both. These are the crossings affected by the PCTN element:

    A*B*PCTN
    A*ALL*PCTN
    ALL*B*PCTN
    ALL*ALL*PCTN

Because C is not crossed with PCTN, it is not included in the denominator definition.

- To obtain the percentage of the value in one table cell to the total for the **column containing the cell**, use all class variables that define the **row** as the denominator definition. For example, the following TABLE statement produces percentages for column totals:

```
PROC TABULATE;
    CLASS A C;
    VAR Y;
    TABLE A,C*Y*PCTN<A>;
```

- To obtain the percentage of the value in one table cell to the total for the **row containing the cell**, use all class variables that define the **column** as the denominator definition. For example, the following TABLE statement produces percentages for row totals:

```
PROC TABULATE;
    CLASS A C;
    VAR Y;
    TABLE A,C*Y*PCTN<C>;
```

(continued on next page)

(continued from previous page)

- To obtain the percentage of the value in one table cell to the total for the **page containing the cell**, cross the class variables that define the **rows and columns of the page** to form the denominator definition. For example, the following TABLE statement produces percentages for page totals:

```
PROC TABULATE;
   CLASS A B C;
   VAR Y;
   TABLE A,B,C*Y*PCTN<B*C>;
```

Chapter 5
Controlling the Table's Appearance

Tables produced by PROC TABULATE convey more information when headings and the values in the table cells are tailored to convey specific types of data. You can

- use formats and labels to modify the values in the table cells and the headings
- control spacing and column widths
- change the appearance of the table outlines.

TABULATE allows you to modify individual components of the table to present output in clear, concise detail.

Recommended Use

New users: work through this chapter to learn step-by-step how to tailor the appearance of tables.

Experienced users: refer to the chapter table of contents for topics of special interest to you.

Contents

Table

Figures

PAGE, ROW, AND COLUMN HEADINGS

PROC TABULATE creates page, row, and column headings that label and describe the contents of the cells printed in the table. As discussed in Chapter 4, "Learning to Use PROC TABULATE," the cells of the table contain summary information about the various categories created by the TABLE statement. The headings for the table reflect the hierarchical relationships of the categories.

How PROC TABULATE Creates Headings

When you issue a TABLE statement with no special instructions for creating headings, PROC TABULATE creates page, row, and column headings from variable names and values and keywords for statistics. Class variables have two levels of headings:

- the variable name
- the variable values.

In creating default headings, TABULATE uses both the name and the values of class variables to define a category. Remember that categories are created for each unique combination of values for class variables.

For analysis variables PROC TABULATE creates headings from the variable name. The values for analysis variables do not appear in headings because they are used to calculate the information in the cells of the table.

The heading for the statistic reported by a table cell is the keyword for the statistic. By default, statistic headings appear in the same dimension as the analysis variables (if your table has analysis variables), although you can request the statistic headings in other dimensions.

When two elements are crossed in a dimension, the element that occurs first in the TABLE statement appears as the first element in the heading for that dimension. That is, the first element in a column dimension crossing is at the top of column headings; the first element in a row dimension crossing is on the far left of row headings; the first element in a page dimension crossing appears in the first set of pages.

The example below illustrates headings for class variables, analysis variables, and the default statistics produced for each of these:

```
DATA STOCKS;
    INPUT STOCK $ TYPE $ EXCHANGE $ SHARES CUSTOMER $ SSN;
    CARDS;
ATT      P NYSE 3   JONES  123456789
HRSHY    C NYSE 50  JONES  123456789
ALCOA    C AMEX 40  JONES  123456789
VOLVO    C OTC  90  JONES  123456789
ITT      C NYSE 35  JONES  123456789
ITT      P NYSE 2   SMITH  987654321
BRENDLE  C OTC  30  SMITH  987654321
ALCOA    P AMEX 1   SMITH  987654321
WANG     C AMEX 20  WHITE  876543210
HRSHY    C NYSE 14  WHITE  876543210
;
PROC TABULATE DATA=STOCKS FORMAT=9.;
    CLASS STOCK TYPE EXCHANGE CUSTOMER SSN;
    VAR SHARES;
    TABLE CUSTOMER,EXCHANGE*STOCK,SHARES TYPE;
RUN;
```

The headings for the first page of output produced by this TABULATE step are illustrated in **Figure 5.1.**† The class variable, CUSTOMER, appears in the page dimension. Note that the heading for this page of the table is the variable name, CUSTOMER, followed by the first value of the variable, JONES. The row dimension headings describe two crossed class variables: EXCHANGE and STOCK. Note how the values for stock are nested within each value of EXCHANGE. The column dimension has headings for both an analysis variable, SHARES, and the class variable, TYPE, which has nested headings for the two values of TYPE: C and P. In addition to the variable headings, this part of the table also has the headings for the statistics reported in the table: SUM and N.

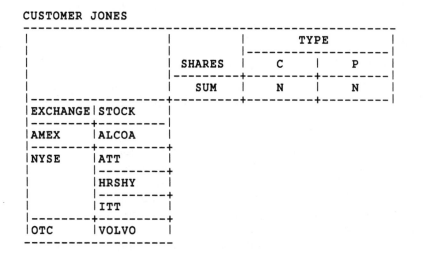

Figure 5.1   Default Headings for Statistics and Variables

The example below has class variables, CUSTOMER and STOCK, in the page and column dimensions and an analysis variable, SHARES, in the row dimension:

```
PROC TABULATE DATA=STOCKS FORMAT=9.;
    CLASS CUSTOMER STOCK;
    VAR SHARES;
    TABLE CUSTOMER,SHARES,STOCK;
RUN;
```

Remember that statistics appear in the same dimension as the analysis variables by default; you must specifically request to print them elsewhere. Refer to **Crossing variables and statistics** in Chapter 4 for more information.

The headings produced by this code are illustrated in **Figure 5.2.**

---

† Many of the examples in this section use the FORMAT= option in the PROC TABULATE statement and the RTS= option in the TABLE statement. These options are needed to produce sample tables that fit in the width of the page. For more information on the FORMAT= option, refer to **Changing Default Formats**. For more information on the RTS= option, refer to **Varying the spacing for row headings with the RTS= option.**

Throughout this section of the chapter, portions of the tables produced by TABULATE are removed to emphasize the portions that are being discussed.

```
CUSTOMER JONES
-------------------------------------------------------------------------
|                        |                     STOCK                     |
|                        |----------------------------------------------|
|                        | ALCOA  |  ATT  | HRSHY  |  ITT  | VOLVO  |
|------------------------+--------+-------+--------+-------+--------|
|SHARES   |SUM  |        |
-------------------------
```

Figure 5.2   Default Placement of Statistic Heading

Changing Default Headings

The tables that PROC TABULATE produces use variable names, values of class variables, and keywords for statistics as page, row, and column headings. If the input data set has formats or labels associated with some variables, TABULATE automatically uses these to make table headings more descriptive.

You can alter the headings for tables produced by PROC TABULATE in a number of ways. You can

- override the default headings by using a data set that has labels and formats assigned to the variables
- use the FORMAT statement to substitute more descriptive headings for class variable values
- specify user-defined formats to group class variables into distinctive classes
- use the LABEL statement to temporarily assign labels to variables
- directly assign a label to a variable name, keyword for a statistic, or ALL in the TABLE statement
- remove some levels of headings that are unnecessary
- use the KEYLABEL statement to assign descriptive labels to ALL or any keywords for statistics.

Each of these techniques for tailoring output is discussed below.

Labels and formats in the input data set

The simplest method for changing the default headings used by PROC TABULATE is to associate labels and formats with the data in the input data set. PROC TABULATE automatically replaces the variable name with the label associated with the variable. TABULATE also formats values of class variables with the associated formats.†

Compare the output in the two examples in **Figures 5.3** and **5.4**. The first prints a table with default table headings. The second example uses the STOCKS data set and adds labels to the SSN, EXCHANGE, and TYPE variables and associates the SSN11. format with the SSN variable. Without changing the code for the PROC TABULATE step, you can produce different table headings by using an input data set with labels and formats.

This PROC TABULATE step produces the default headings:

```
PROC TABULATE DATA=STOCKS FORMAT=9.;
   CLASS STOCK TYPE EXCHANGE CUSTOMER SSN;
   TABLE SSN,EXCHANGE*TYPE / RTS=13;
RUN;
```

---

† Formatting class variables is most useful with user-defined formats. Refer to **Formatting headings of class variables** for more information on user-defined formats.

The headings produced by this code are illustrated in **Figure 5.3**.

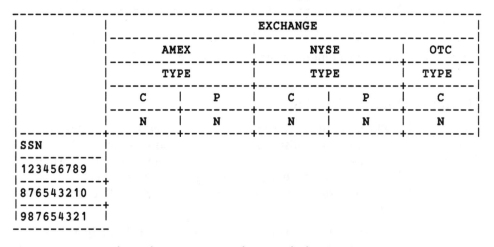

Figure 5.3 Headings for Data Set with No Labels or Formats

The following DATA step adds labels and formats to the STOCKS data set. You would typically add labels and formats at the time you first create a data set, but this code adds them in a separate DATA step to illustrate how TABULATE uses variables that have labels and formats assigned to them. The code for the PROC TABULATE step is unchanged.

```
DATA FANCY;
   SET STOCKS;
   FORMAT SSN SSN11.;
   LABEL SSN='Customer''s SSN'
         EXCHANGE='Exchange'
         TYPE='Type of Stock';
PROC TABULATE DATA=FANCY FORMAT=9.;
   CLASS TYPE EXCHANGE SSN;
   TABLE SSN,EXCHANGE*TYPE / RTS=13;
RUN;
```

Although the TABULATE coding has not changed from the last example, the table in **Figure 5.4** differs from the table in **Figure 5.3** because labels replace variable names, and formatted values for the SSN variable replace unformatted values.

```
|           |                       Exchange                        |
|           |---------------------------------------------|---------|
|           |                   |                   |         OTC     |
|           |      AMEX         |      NYSE         |---------|
|           |-------------------|-------------------| Type of |
|           |  Type of Stock    |  Type of Stock    |  Stock  |
|           |-------------------|-------------------|---------|
|           |  C   |    P       |  C   |    P       |    C    |
|           |------+------------+------+------------+---------|
|           |  N   |    N       |  N   |    N       |    N    |
|-----------+------+------------+------+------------+---------|
|Customer's |
|SSN        |
|-----------|
|123-45-6789|
|-----------+
|876-54-3210|
|-----------+
|987-65-4321|
-------------
```

Figure 5.4   Headings for Data Set with Labels and Formats

Formatting headings of class variables

In many cases, you want to use formats to change headings for class variables, but you do not want to permanently associate these formats with the variables in the SAS data set. The FORMAT statement allows you to temporarily associate SAS formats or user-defined formats with class variables for the duration of the PROC TABULATE step. Refer to **Figure 5.8** for an illustration of using SAS formats in the FORMAT statement.† The remainder of this topic discusses how to create and use your own formats as temporary headings for class variables.

One of the most important reasons for specifying a user-defined format is to group values into different classes. For example, if your data set has an AGE variable with values in the range of 1 to 70, and you use AGE as a class variable in a TABULATE step, the table produced by TABULATE has up to 70 columns or rows for the AGE variable!

By creating a user-defined format that groups values of class variables and specifying the format in the TABULATE step that prints the table, you can create more meaningful headings to describe the columns and rows, and at the same time, greatly reduce the number of columns or rows for a variable.‡

The example in **Figure 5.5** uses the AGE variable described above to illustrate how user-defined formats can create classes. This example groups people who responded to an ad survey into five age categories. The example uses PROC FORMAT to create a temporary user-defined format, AGEFMT. When this format is specified in the PROC TABULATE step, TABULATE groups the values of the AGE variable into the classes defined by AGEFMT. This reduces the number of class values and produces a more meaningful report.

```
PROC FORMAT;
   VALUE AGEFMT 0-29 ='UNDER 30'
                30-39='30-39'
                40-49='40-49'
                50-70='50-70'
                OTHER='OVER 70';
```

---

† For a complete list of SAS formats, refer to the *SAS User's Guide: Basics, Version 5 Edition* or *SAS Language Guide for Personal Computers, Version 6 Edition*.

‡ Refer to "Details of TABULATE Processing" for a more detailed discussion of setting up useful classes.

```
PROC TABULATE DATA=ADSURVEY;
   FORMAT AGE AGEFMT.;
   CLASS SEX AGE;
   VAR   AD1 AD2 AD3;
   TABLE SEX*AGE,
         MEAN*(AD1 AD2 AD3);
RUN;
```

The headings produced by this code follow.

```
------------------------------------------------------------
|          |        |               MEAN                   |
|          |        |--------------------------------------|
|          |        |   AD1    |    AD2    |    AD3   |
|----------+--------+----------+-----------+-----------|
|SEX       |AGE     |
|----------+--------|
|F         |UNDER   |
|          |30      |
|          |--------+
|          |30-39   |
|          |--------+
|          |40-49   |
|          |--------+
|          |50-70   |
|          |--------+
|          |OVER 70 |
|----------+--------+
|M         |UNDER   |
|          |30      |
|          |--------+
|          |30-39   |
|          |--------+
|          |40-49   |
|          |--------+
|          |50-70   |
|          |--------+
|          |OVER 70 |
------------------------
```

Figure 5.5   Formatted Headings for Class Variables

Keep in mind several important points about using formatted values for class variables in PROC TABULATE:

- User-defined formats, which you create by using PROC FORMAT, are a good method for grouping values of class variables into meaningful categories.
- You must specify a FORMAT statement in the PROC TABULATE step to make use of SAS formats or user-defined formats unless the format is permanently associated with the variable in the SAS data set.
- If no values occur in the data set for one of the groups defined by a format, PROC TABULATE does **not** print a heading for that group.
- TABULATE prints nested row and column headings for only the categories that occur for those crossings, unless the PRINTMISS option is specified.

The last point is illustrated by the output in **Figure 5.6**. This example introduces another format that groups respondents by income, as well as age. This example separates the data illustrated in **Figure 5.5** into three income levels and prints a separate page for each income level. For some of the age groups within a specific income level there are no observations in the data set. Thus, the first page of the report (which reports responses of people who did not provide income information) has no row for females age 40 to 49 or over 70, or for males under 30 or 40 to 49. The other two pages of the report have rows for all age groups for both sexes.

```
PROC FORMAT;
   VALUE AGEFMT 0-29 ='UNDER 30'
                30-39='30-39'
                40-49='40-49'
                50-70='50-70'
                OTHER='OVER 70';
   VALUE INCFMT . ='NO ANSWER'
                0-24999='UNDER 25,000'
                OTHER='25,000 OR MORE';
PROC TABULATE DATA=ADSURVEY MISSING;
   FORMAT INCOME INCFMT. AGE AGEFMT.;
   CLASS INCOME SEX AGE;
   VAR   AD1 AD2 AD3;
   TABLE INCOME,SEX*AGE,
         MEAN*(AD1 AD2 AD3);
RUN;
```

The headings produced by this code follow.

```
INCOME NO ANSWER
----------------------------------------------------------------
|           |           |                MEAN                  |
|           |           |--------------------------------------|
|           |           |  AD1     |   AD2     |   AD3          |
|-----------+-----------+----------+-----------+----------------|
|SEX   |AGE |
|------+-----|
|F     |UNDER |
|      |30    |
|      |------+
|      |30-39 |
|      |------+
|      |50-70 |
|------+-----+
|M     |30-39 |
|      |------+
|      |50-70 |
|      |------+
|      |OVER 70|
----------------
```

(Figure continued on next page)

```
INCOME UNDER 25,000
-------------------------------------------------------------
|              |                    MEAN                     |
|              |---------------------------------------------|
|              |    AD1     |    AD2     |    AD3            |
|--------------+------------+------------+-----------|
|SEX    |AGE   |
|-------+------|
|F      |UNDER |
|       |30    |
|       |------+
|       |30-39 |
|       |------+
|       |40-49 |
|       |------+
|       |50-70 |
|       |------+
|       |OVER 70|
|-------+------+
|M      |UNDER |
|       |30    |
|       |------+
|       |30-39 |
|       |------+
|       |40-49 |
|       |------+
|       |50-70 |
|       |------+
|       |OVER 70|
---------------
```

```
INCOME 25,000 OR MORE
-------------------------------------------------------------
|              |                    MEAN                     |
|              |---------------------------------------------|
|              |    AD1     |    AD2     |    AD3            |
|--------------+------------+------------+-----------|
|SEX    |AGE   |
|-------+------|
|F      |UNDER |
|       |30    |
|       |------+
|       |30-39 |
|       |------+
|       |40-49 |
|       |------+
|       |50-70 |
|       |------+
|       |OVER 70|
|-------+------+
|M      |UNDER |
|       |30    |
|       |------+
|       |30-39 |
|       |------+
|       |40-49 |
|       |------+
|       |50-70 |
|       |------+
|       |OVER 70|
---------------
```

Figure 5.6   Nonuniform Headings for Multiple-Page Table

When the PRINTMISS option is added to the TABLE statement, the headings for each page of output are the same. The following TABULATE step is the same as the one that produced **Figure 5.6** except the PRINTMISS option has been added to the TABLE statement. Note how the headings on the first page of this output, illustrated in **Figure 5.7**, differ from the headings on the first page of **Figure 5.6**.

```
PROC TABULATE DATA=ADSURVEY MISSING;
   FORMAT INCOME INCFMT. AGE AGEFMT.;
   CLASS INCOME SEX AGE;
   VAR   AD1 AD2 AD3;
   TABLE INCOME,SEX*AGE,
         MEAN*(AD1 AD2 AD3) / PRINTMISS;
RUN;
```

The first page of the table produced by this code follows. Note that the values appear in the cells of this table to illustrate how TABULATE prints missing values for rows that print only when PRINTMISS is specified.

```
INCOME NO ANSWER
------------------------------------------------------------------
|           |           |              MEAN                      |
|           |           |---------------------------------------|
|           |           |   AD1     |   AD2     |   AD3     |
|-----------+-----------+-----------+-----------+-----------|
|SEX  |AGE  |           |           |           |
|-----+-----|           |           |           |
|F    |UNDER|           |           |           |
|     |30   |     2.00|     2.00|     0.00|
|     |-----+-----------+-----------+-----------|
|     |30-39|     5.00|     1.00|     4.00|
|     |-----+-----------+-----------+-----------|
|     |40-49|       . |       . |       . |
|     |-----+-----------+-----------+-----------|
|     |50-70|     2.50|     5.50|     5.00|
|     |-----+-----------+-----------+-----------|
|     |OVER 70|     . |       . |       . |
|-----+-----+-----------+-----------+-----------|
|M    |UNDER|           |           |           |
|     |30   |       . |       . |       . |
|     |-----+-----------+-----------+-----------|
|     |30-39|     7.00|     0.50|     3.50|
|     |-----+-----------+-----------+-----------|
|     |40-49|       . |       . |       . |
|     |-----+-----------+-----------+-----------|
|     |50-70|     6.00|     2.00|     1.00|
|     |-----+-----------+-----------+-----------|
|     |OVER 70|   9.00|     0.00|     1.00|
------------------------------------------------------------------
```

Figure 5.7   Making Headings Uniform for Multiple-Page Tables

Creating temporary labels for variable names

Labels and formats in the input data set discussed how you can add labels to variables in the input data set to replace the variable name in the output produced by PROC TABULATE. You may also want to replace variable names temporarily without adding labels to the input data set. This can be done by

- using the LABEL statement in the PROC TABULATE step
- assigning a label to an element in the TABLE statement.

Both of these methods are discussed in this section.

The LABEL statement creates a descriptive heading for a variable in procedure output. When this statement is used with PROC TABULATE, the heading for the variable name is replaced by the label. For example, you can produce the same output as illustrated in **Figure 5.4** by temporarily assigning labels to variables instead of adding labels to the input data set. **Figure 5.3** illustrates a simple table that has variables names as headings. The following code modifies that table by using the LABEL statement in the TABULATE step to label each of the three class variables, SSN, EXCHANGE, and TYPE:

```
PROC TABULATE DATA=STOCKS FORMAT=9.;
   CLASS TYPE EXCHANGE SSN;
   VAR SHARES;
   TABLE SSN,EXCHANGE*TYPE / RTS=13;
   FORMAT SSN SSN11.;
   LABEL SSN='Customer''s SSN'
         EXCHANGE='Exchange'
         TYPE='Type of Stock';
RUN;
```

The output in **Figure 5.8** illustrates how the headings are temporarily changed. Note also that the FORMAT statement temporarily assigns the SAS format SSN11. to the values of SSN.

```
-----------------------------------------------------------------
|           |                    Exchange                       |
|           |---------------------------------------------------|
|           |              |              |        | OTC        |
|           |     AMEX     |     NYSE     |        |----------- |
|           |--------------+--------------|        | Type of    |
|           | Type of Stock| Type of Stock|        | Stock      |
|           |--------------+--------------+--------------------- |
|           |  C   |   P   |  C   |   P   |      C              |
|           |------+-------+------+-------+---------------------|
|           |  N   |   N   |  N   |   N   |      N              |
|-----------+------+-------+------+-------+---------------------|
|Customer's |
|SSN        |
|-----------|
|123-45-6789|
|-----------+
|876-54-3210|
|-----------+
|987-65-4321|
-------------
```

Figure 5.8   Using Temporary Labels and Formats for Headings

Assigning labels to variables with the LABEL statement is particularly useful when the PROC TABULATE step contains several TABLE statements that use the same variable. For example, the LABEL statement in the following code produces a descriptive heading for the SHARES variable in both of the tables illustrated in **Figure 5.9**:

```
PROC TABULATE DATA=STOCKS FORMAT=9.;
   CLASS STOCK CUSTOMER TYPE;
   VAR SHARES;
   TABLE STOCK,CUSTOMER*SHARES;
   TABLE STOCK*TYPE,CUSTOMER*SHARES;
   LABEL SHARES='SHARES HELD';
RUN;
```

The headings produced by this code are illustrated below.

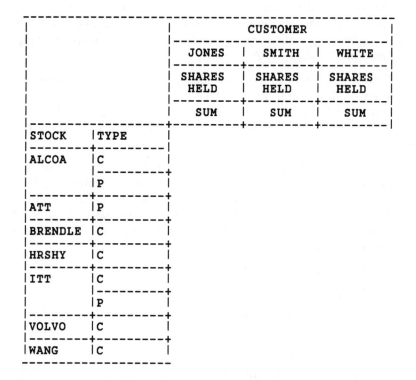

```
-------------------------------------------------------------
|                  |                 CUSTOMER               |
|                  |-----------------------------------------|
|                  | JONES    | SMITH    | WHITE    |
|                  |----------+----------+----------|
|                  | SHARES   | SHARES   | SHARES   |
|                  |  HELD    |  HELD    |  HELD    |
|                  |----------+----------+----------|
|                  |  SUM     |  SUM     |  SUM     |
|------------------+----------+----------+----------|
|STOCK             |
|------------------|
|ALCOA             |
|------------------+
|ATT               |
|------------------+
|BRENDLE           |
|------------------+
|HRSHY             |
|------------------+
|ITT               |
|------------------+
|VOLVO             |
|------------------+
|WANG              |
--------------------
```

```
-------------------------------------------------------------
|                  |                 CUSTOMER               |
|                  |-----------------------------------------|
|                  | JONES    | SMITH    | WHITE    |
|                  |----------+----------+----------|
|                  | SHARES   | SHARES   | SHARES   |
|                  |  HELD    |  HELD    |  HELD    |
|                  |----------+----------+----------|
|                  |  SUM     |  SUM     |  SUM     |
|---------+--------+----------+----------+----------|
|STOCK    |TYPE    |
|---------+--------|
|ALCOA    |C       |
|         |--------+
|         |P       |
|---------+--------+
|ATT      |P       |
|---------+--------+
|BRENDLE  |C       |
|---------+--------+
|HRSHY    |C       |
|---------+--------+
|ITT      |C       |
|         |--------+
|         |P       |
|---------+--------+
|VOLVO    |C       |
|---------+--------+
|WANG     |C       |
--------------------
```

Figure 5.9 Multiple Tables Using the Same LABEL Statement

Another method of replacing variable names with labels is to assign a label in the TABLE statement. For example, the following statements produce the same tables illustrated in **Figure 5.9**, but this time the labels are assigned in the TABLE statement:

```
TABLE STOCK,CUSTOMER*SHARES='SHARES HELD';
TABLE STOCK*TYPE,CUSTOMER*SHARES='SHARES HELD';
```

This method is useful when you want to create a descriptive heading for a single occurrence in the table. The label you assign in a TABLE statement affects only that instance of the variable in the TABLE statement where it appears; it has no effect on other TABLE statements in the TABULATE step or on other occurrences of the same variable in the same TABLE statement.

When you use several methods to define labels for headings, the order of precedence is as follows:

1. The labels that occur in the data set are used as the default heading.
2. Any labels defined in the LABEL statement override those in the data set.
3. Labels assigned in the TABLE statement override both the data set labels and those defined in the LABEL statement.

Changing headings for statistics and ALL

Two common elements in TABULATE headings are the statistics being reported and the group class ALL.† Some tables produced by TABULATE become more meaningful if you replace the statistic or ALL with a more descriptive heading. To replace headings for statistics and ALL, you can

- use the KEYLABEL statement to assign a descriptive label that replaces each occurrence of the term in the TABULATE step.
- assign a descriptive label in the TABLE statement to replace a single occurrence of the term. This type of label overrides the label defined in a KEYLABEL statement.

If you are producing a report that lists the sum of values for an analysis variable, you may want to replace the SUM statistic label with a more descriptive heading. Consider the report illustrated in **Figure 5.10**. The SUM statistic in this report has been replaced by the label # HELD. The TABLE statement requests that the SUM statistic appear in the column dimension. Note that the KEYLABEL statement causes all occurrences of SUM to be replaced by # HELD.‡

```
PROC TABULATE DATA=STOCKS FORMAT=9.;
   CLASS STOCK CUSTOMER;
   VAR SHARES;
   TABLE CUSTOMER,SHARES,STOCK*SUM / RTS=12;
   KEYLABEL SUM='# HELD';
RUN;
```

The headings produced by this code follow.

---

† For crossings involving only class variables, the statistic is the frequency, N, or the percentage of frequency, PCTN. When the crossing includes analysis variables, many other statistics can be requested. Refer to **STATISTICS AVAILABLE WITH PROC TABULATE** in Chapter 2 for a complete description of the available statistics.

‡ Refer to **Rearranging the TABLE Statement to Improve Headings** for a different method of constructing headings that reduces the repetition.

```
CUSTOMER JONES
-------------------------------------------------------------------
|          |                       STOCK                           |
|          |---------------------------------------------------------|
|          |  ALCOA  |   ATT   |  HRSHY  |   ITT   |  VOLVO  |
|          |---------+---------+---------+---------+---------|
|          | # HELD  | # HELD  | # HELD  | # HELD  | # HELD  |
|          |---------+---------+---------+---------+---------|
|SHARES    |
----------
```

Figure 5.10   Replacing the Heading for the Statistic

Removing levels of headings

There are times when the multiple levels of headings for class and analysis variables are not necessary in your tables. This often occurs when you replace a default heading with more descriptive text that actually includes the information in two levels of heading. For example, the simple table created by the following code reports the SUM statistic for an analysis variable.

```
PROC TABULATE DATA=STOCKS FORMAT=9.;
   CLASS TYPE STOCK;
   VAR SHARES;
   TABLE SHARES;
RUN;
```

This table has the headings illustrated in **Figure 5.11**.

```
-----------
| SHARES  |
|---------|
|  SUM    |
|---------|
|     285 |
-----------
```

Figure 5.11   Default Heading for Analysis Variable and Statistic

You can simplify these headings by removing one of the headings and redefining the existing heading with a new label. This TABLE statement

```
TABLE SHARES='NUMBER OF SHARES'*SUM=' ';
```

produces a single level of heading, illustrated in **Figure 5.12**.

```
-----------
|NUMBER OF|
| SHARES  |
|---------|
|     285 |
-----------
```

Figure 5.12   Removing a Level of Heading

Removing levels of headings is useful for any type of heading you can define in a TABULATE procedure. You can assign blank headings to keywords or variable names in the TABLE statement. You can also replace headings for keywords for statistics or ALL by specifying blanks in the KEYLABEL statement. Keep in mind that the form for removing a heading in a KEYLABEL statement or in the TABLE statement is

```
element=' ';
```

At least one blank is required between the quotation marks. If you omit the blank, the heading is replaced with a single quotation mark. Note: you cannot remove headings for a class variable name by assigning a blank label in the LABEL statement. You must assign blank headings to variable names in the TABLE statement.

Rearranging the TABLE Statement to Improve Headings

The order in which levels appear in headings depends upon the structure of the TABLE statement. As discussed in Chapter 4, "Learning to Use PROC TABULATE," the page, row, and column dimensions of the table are defined in that order. In addition, within each of these dimensions the order in which you specify the elements determines the appearance of the headings. Rearranging the TABLE statement can improve the appearance of tables by allowing you to

- emphasize different variables by placing them at higher or lower levels of heading
- avoid repetition
- gain more space for descriptive headings.

The simplest method of rearranging a TABLE statement is to reorder crossings within a single dimension of the table. For example, **Figure 5.13** illustrates two simple one-dimensional tables that use the class variables, TYPE and CUSTOMER. Note the different headings in the table that result from reversing the order of the crossing of TYPE and CUSTOMER. Note also that the same values are produced, but they occur in different columns.

```
PROC TABULATE DATA=STOCKS FORMAT=6.;
   CLASS CUSTOMER TYPE;
   TABLE CUSTOMER*TYPE;
   TABLE TYPE*CUSTOMER;
RUN;
```

The tables produced by this code follow.

```
-----------------------------------------------------------------
|                            CUSTOMER                            |
|---------------------------------------------------------------|
|         JONES          |          SMITH         |   WHITE      |
|---------------------------------------------------------------|
|         TYPE           |          TYPE          |   TYPE       |
|---------------------------------------------------------------|
|    C    |    P         |    C    |    P         |    C         |
|---------+--------------+---------+--------------+--------------|
|    N    |    N         |    N    |    N         |    N         |
|---------+--------------+---------+--------------+--------------|
|       4 |          1   |       1 |          2   |          2   |
-----------------------------------------------------------------
```

```
-----------------------------------------------------------------
|                             TYPE                              |
|---------------------------------------------------------------|
|             C                |              P                |
|---------------------------------------------------------------|
|          CUSTOMER            |           CUSTOMER            |
|---------------------------------------------------------------|
| JONES  |  SMITH  |  WHITE    |  JONES   |   SMITH            |
|--------+---------+-----------+----------+-------------------|
|   N    |    N    |    N      |    N     |    N               |
|--------+---------+-----------+----------+-------------------|
|      4 |       1 |        2  |       1  |        2           |
-----------------------------------------------------------------
```

Figure 5.13   Rearranging the Order of Headings

The same type of ordering occurs in the row dimension as well as the column dimension. That is, the element that is specified first in the row dimension appears as the heading on the far left of the table; the element specified first in the column dimension appears as the top heading.

You can also rearrange the levels of heading for a single variable. If you specify a class variable in the column dimension of a TABLE statement and do not explicitly specify a statistic in the statement, the default order of headings is the variable name first, the variable values next, and the statistic last. You can rearrange these headings to reduce repetition. If you refer to the example in **Figure 5.10**, you see the headings for the column dimension appear in this order:

- variable name (STOCK)
- variable value (ALCOA, ATT, HRSHY, ITT, VOLVO)
- statistic (relabeled as # HELD).

Note that in **Figure 5.10**, the statistic is repeated for each variable value. This is often useful when several statistics are reported for each variable, but in this case, the appearance of the table would be improved by removing the repetition.

The output illustrated in **Figure 5.14** reorders the levels of headings to remove the repetition. The new order also permits more space for the label substituted for SUM, so the more descriptive label NUMBER OF SHARES HELD can be used instead of # HELD.

```
PROC TABULATE DATA=STOCKS FORMAT=7.;
   CLASS STOCK CUSTOMER;
   VAR SHARES;
   TABLE SUM*STOCK*SHARES=' ';
   KEYLABEL SUM='NUMBER OF SHARES HELD';
RUN;
```

The headings produced by this code follow.

```
------------------------------------------------------------
|                  NUMBER OF SHARES HELD                   |
|----------------------------------------------------------|
|                         STOCK                            |
|----------------------------------------------------------|
| ALCOA |  ATT  |BRENDLE| HRSHY |  ITT  | VOLVO | WANG  |
|-------+-------+-------+-------+-------+-------+-------|
```

Figure 5.14 Eliminating Repetition from Headings

Controlling the Spacing in Headings

This section discusses the TABLE statement option that permits you to tailor the spacing of headings and also describes how TABULATE splits headings within row and column spacing. Note: to control the width of column headings, you must also change the width of the table cells. Refer to **Controlling the Width of Columns** for information on spacing in column headings.

Varying the spacing for row headings with the RTS= option

By default, TABULATE calculates the width of row headings to be one-quarter of the value of the LINESIZE= system option. The first and last spaces in the row heading are used for the table outlining character, so the actual space for printing row headings can be calculated with this formula:

(LINESIZE / 4) − 2 .

Thus, if you specify LINESIZE=80 in the OPTIONS statement, TABULATE allows 18 spaces for printing row headings. This amount of space may or may not be appropriate for your table. If you need to vary the row title spacing, use the RTS= option in the TABLE statement. For example, compare the output in **Figure 5.15**, which uses the default row heading spacing, to the output in **Figure 5.16**, which specifies RTS=10.

```
OPTIONS LS=80;
PROC TABULATE DATA=STOCKS FORMAT=9.;
   CLASS CUSTOMER TYPE;
   VAR SHARES;
   TABLE CUSTOMER,TYPE*SHARES;
RUN;
```

The space for printing the row headings illustrated in **Figure 5.15** is twenty: eighteen for the text of the heading and two for the vertical dividers.

```
----------------------------------------------------
|                   |            TYPE            |
|                   |----------------------------|
|                   |    C     |      P     |
|                   |----------+-----------|
|                   |  SHARES  |   SHARES   |
|                   |----------+-----------|
|                   |   SUM    |    SUM     |
|-------------------+----------+-----------|
|CUSTOMER           |
|-------------------|
|JONES              |
|-------------------+
|SMITH              |
|-------------------+
|WHITE              |
--------------------
```

Figure 5.15 Default Row Title Space

The space for printing the text of the row headings in **Figure 5.16** has been reduced to 8 by the RTS=10 option. The remaining two spaces are used for the vertical dividers.

```
OPTIONS LS=80;
PROC TABULATE DATA=STOCKS FORMAT=9.;
   CLASS CUSTOMER TYPE;
   VAR SHARES;
   TABLE CUSTOMER,TYPE*SHARES / RTS=10;
RUN;
```

```
---------------------------------
|          |          TYPE       |
|          |---------------------|
|          |    C     |    P     |
|          |----------+----------|
|          |  SHARES  |  SHARES  |
|          |----------+----------|
|          |   SUM    |   SUM    |
|----------+----------+----------|
|CUSTOMER  |
|----------|
|JONES     |
|----------+
|SMITH     |
|----------+
|WHITE     |
-----------
```

Figure 5.16   Tailored Row Title Space

Keep in mind that the amount of space you specify for the RTS= option is divided evenly among all headings in the row dimension. Note the amount of space for the two levels of heading in **Figure 5.17**. The RTS= option in the following code has the value 17:

```
PROC TABULATE DATA=STOCKS FORMAT=9.;
   CLASS STOCK TYPE;
   VAR SHARES;
   TABLE STOCK*TYPE,SHARES / RTS=17;
RUN;
```

and the width of each row heading is 7. The remaining 3 spaces of the RTS= value are used for the dividing lines.

```
-----------------------------------
|                |  SHARES   |
|                |---------- |
|                |  SUM      |
|----------------+---------- |
|STOCK    |TYPE  |
|-------- +------|
|ALCOA    |C     |
|         |------|
|         |P     |
|-------- +------+
|ATT      |P     |
|-------- +------+
|BRENDLE  |C     |
|-------- +------+
|HRSHY    |C     |
|-------- +------+
|ITT      |C     |
|         |------+
|         |P     |
|-------- +------+
|VOLVO    |C     |
|-------- +------+
|WANG     |C     |
-----------------------------------
```

Figure 5.17   Headings for Variables Crossed in the Row Dimension

How PROC TABULATE splits headings

TABULATE automatically splits the text for headings to fit the space allotted. TABULATE looks for a blank or hyphen in the heading and splits the text there if possible. If a single word does not fit within the space for the heading, TABULATE prints as much of the word as will fit, inserts a hyphen in the last space, and continues the word on the next line. You can force TABULATE to split a word at a specific place in the word by inserting a hyphen in the word. Please note, however, that if the space provided for headings changes and the entire word can fit on the line without splitting it, TABULATE does **not** automatically remove the hyphen.

Page Titles

You can define titles for TABULATE output as you can for all SAS procedures by using the TITLE statement. The tables produced by PROC TABULATE have an additional page heading when a page dimension is included in the TABLE statement. As for all headings in TABULATE output, the page heading consists of variable names, values, and statistics.

In addition to modifying the contents of the page heading as you do for row and column headings, you can change the location of page headings on the page.† By default, page headings are printed above the table on the left side. The BOX= option allows you to move the page heading into the top left box of the table or insert either a variable name (or label) or a descriptive string in the box.

You can use the BOX= option in a three-dimensional table to place the page heading in the box. **Figure 5.18** illustrates how the coding for **Figure 5.6** can be modified to create automatic box headings from the page dimension. The only

---

† Refer to **Changing Default Headings** for more details.

change to the coding is the addition of the BOX= option in the TABLE statement.

```
PROC TABULATE DATA=ADSURVEY MISSING;
   FORMAT INCOME INCFMT. AGE AGEFMT.;
   CLASS INCOME SEX AGE;
   VAR  AD1 AD2 AD3;
   TABLE INCOME,SEX*AGE,
         MEAN*(AD1 AD2 AD3)
         / BOX=_PAGE_;
RUN;
```

The page headings produced by this code appear in the page box.†

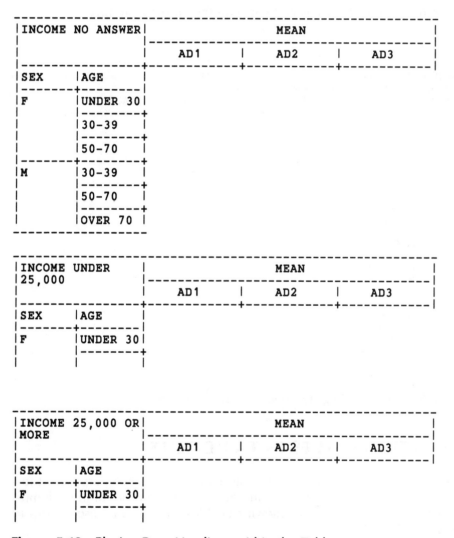

Figure 5.18 Placing Page Headings within the Table

You can also create a descriptive heading for the table even when you do not use a page dimension in the TABLE statement. Simply use the BOX= option to

---

insert a descriptive string into the box. **Figure 5.19** modifies the coding for **Figure 5.5** to illustrate how to use the BOX= option to place a heading in a table that has only two dimensions. Note: the only change to the TABULATE step is the addition of the BOX= option in the TABLE statement.

```
PROC TABULATE DATA=ADSURVEY MISSING;
   FORMAT AGE AGEFMT.;
   CLASS SEX AGE;
   VAR   AD1 AD2 AD3;
   TABLE SEX*AGE,
         MEAN*(AD1 AD2 AD3)
         / BOX='RESPONSES BY SEX AND AGE FOR ALL INCOMES';
RUN;
```

The headings produced by this code include text in the page box.

```
----------------------------------------------------------------------
|RESPONSES BY SEX|                        MEAN                       |
|AND AGE FOR ALL |-----------------------------------------------------|
|INCOMES         |    AD1     |    AD2     |    AD3     |
|----------------+------------+------------+------------|
|SEX     |AGE    |
|--------+-------|
|F       |UNDER 30|
|        |--------+
|        |30-39  |
|        |--------+
|        |40-49  |
|        |--------+
|        |50-70  |
|        |--------+
|        |OVER 70 |
|--------+--------+
|M       |UNDER 30|
|        |--------+
|        |30-39  |
|        |--------+
|        |40-49  |
|        |--------+
|        |50-70  |
|        |--------+
|        |OVER 70 |
-----------------
```

Figure 5.19   Page Headings for Two-Dimensional Tables

FORMATTING VALUES IN TABLE CELLS

Specifying the format for data in table cells actually serves two purposes. It formats the values that print in the cells and determines the width of the columns.

   The data set generated by the following DATA step is used to discuss how to format values in table cells:

```
DATA DONORS;
   INPUT SEX $ BLDTYPE $ RHFACTOR $ HEMOGLOB;
   CARDS;
M AB + 14.9
M A  + 15.3
M A  + 16.2
```

```
F O   + 12.
F O   - 15.6
M A   + 15.
M A   + 18.
F O   + 13.2
M B   + 14.9
F A   + 12.1
F A   + 14.3
M A   + 17.8
M O   + 15.4
F O   + 15.9
F O   + 15.5
F A   + 13.
M A   + 15.6
M O   + 14.3
F B   + 15.6
F O   - 12.4
M A   + 17.8
M O   + 15.
M AB  - 13.9
M O   + 18.
F O   + 13.1
F A   - 12.5
M O   + 14.
M B   - 16.2
;
RUN;
```

Why Format Table Cells?

The default format for table cells is useful for many types of reports printed by PROC TABULATE, but there are times when the information in a report is clearer if the report is formatted differently. To illustrate the usefulness of formatting values in individual table cells, **Figures 5.20** through **5.22** show the same report as it changes from all default formats to specific formats for each type of data in the table cells. Note: these examples are not discussed in detail; they are provided only to illustrate the usefulness of formatting. The remainder of this section provides detailed information on formatting tables in the page, row, and column dimensions.

Figure 5.20 shows a report that provides the mean, minimum, and maximum of hemoglobin counts for each blood type and the frequency of each blood type by sex. This report uses the default format, 12.2, so each column has a width of 12. Note that the report requires two pages because the columns are too wide to fit within the line size.

```
PROC TABULATE DATA=DONORS;
   CLASS SEX BLDTYPE RHFACTOR;
   VAR HEMOGLOB;
   TABLE BLDTYPE*RHFACTOR,HEMOGLOB*(MEAN MIN MAX) SEX;
RUN;
```

This code produces the following output.

```
-----------------------------------------------------------------
|                     |                    HEMOGLOB             |
|                     |------------------------------------------|
|                     |    MEAN    |    MIN     |    MAX       |
|---------------------+------------+------------+--------------|
|BLDTY- |RHFACT-|      |            |            |              |
|PE     |OR     |      |            |            |              |
|-------+-------|      |            |            |              |
|A      |+      |        15.51|       12.10|         18.00|
|       |-------+------------+------------+--------------|
|       |-      |        12.50|       12.50|         12.50|
|-------+-------+------------+------------+--------------|
|AB     |+      |        14.90|       14.90|         14.90|
|       |-------+------------+------------+--------------|
|       |-      |        13.90|       13.90|         13.90|
|-------+-------+------------+------------+--------------|
|B      |+      |        15.25|       14.90|         15.60|
|       |-------+------------+------------+--------------|
|       |-      |        16.20|       16.20|         16.20|
|-------+-------+------------+------------+--------------|
|O      |+      |        14.64|       12.00|         18.00|
|       |-------+------------+------------+--------------|
|       |-      |        14.00|       12.40|         15.60|
-----------------------------------------------------------------
```

(CONTINUED)

```
---------------------------------------------------------
|                     |               SEX              |
|                     |---------------------------------|
|                     |     F      |     M            |
|                     |------------+--------------------|
|                     |     N      |     N            |
|---------------------+------------+-------------------|
|BLDTY- |RHFACT-|      |            |                  |
|PE     |OR     |      |            |                  |
|-------+-------|      |            |                  |
|A      |+      |         3.00|        7.00|
|       |-------+------------+-------------------|
|       |-      |         1.00|           .|
|-------+-------+------------+-------------------|
|AB     |+      |            .|        1.00|
|       |-------+------------+-------------------|
|       |-      |            .|        1.00|
|-------+-------+------------+-------------------|
|B      |+      |         1.00|        1.00|
|       |-------+------------+-------------------|
|       |-      |            .|        1.00|
|-------+-------+------------+-------------------|
|O      |+      |         5.00|        5.00|
|       |-------+------------+-------------------|
|       |-      |         2.00|           .|
---------------------------------------------------------
```

Figure 5.20   Default Formatting of Table Cells

The first step in modifying the report is to reduce the width of the columns. This step is often necessary when the report spans more than the width of the page. By reducing the width of each column, more columns fit on the page. Of course, you must be sure that the column width you specify allows PROC TABULATE to express the values in the table cell adequately. **Figure 5.21** shows the output when the default format is changed to 8.1 with the FORMAT= option in the PROC TABULATE statement. Making the columns narrower also allows you to expand the space for the row headings by using the RTS= option.

```
PROC TABULATE DATA=DONORS FORMAT=8.1 ;
   CLASS SEX BLDTYPE RHFACTOR;
   VAR HEMOGLOB;
   TABLE BLDTYPE*RHFACTOR,HEMOGLOB*(MEAN MIN MAX) SEX / RTS=18 ;
RUN;
```

This code produces the following output.

		HEMOGLOB			SEX	
					F	M
		MEAN	MIN	MAX	N	N
BLDTYPE	RHFACTOR					
A	+	15.5	12.1	18.0	3.0	7.0
	-	12.5	12.5	12.5	1.0	.
AB	+	14.9	14.9	14.9	.	1.0
	-	13.9	13.9	13.9	.	1.0
B	+	15.2	14.9	15.6	1.0	1.0
	-	16.2	16.2	16.2	.	1.0
O	+	14.6	12.0	18.0	5.0	5.0
	-	14.0	12.4	15.6	2.0	.

Figure 5.21 Changing the Width of Table Cells

Finally, some groups of cells may need to be formatted separately to make the table more meaningful. For example, the number of donors for each sex would be better represented with no decimal places and would require less space. **Figure 5.22** formats the frequency values using the 4. format.

```
PROC TABULATE DATA=DONORS FORMAT=8.1 ;
   CLASS SEX BLDTYPE RHFACTOR;
   VAR HEMOGLOB;
   TABLE BLDTYPE*RHFACTOR,HEMOGLOB*(MEAN MIN MAX) SEX*F=4. / RTS=18 ;
RUN;
```

This code produces the following output.

BLDTYPE	RHFACTOR	HEMOGLOB			SEX	
		MEAN	MIN	MAX	F	M
					N	N
A	+	15.5	12.1	18.0	3	7
	−	12.5	12.5	12.5	1	.
AB	+	14.9	14.9	14.9	.	1
	−	13.9	13.9	13.9	.	1
B	+	15.2	14.9	15.6	1	1
	−	16.2	16.2	16.2	.	1
O	+	14.6	12.0	18.0	5	5
	−	14.0	12.4	15.6	2	.

Figure 5.22   Changing the Format of Selected Table Cells

Changing Default Formats

The default format for values in table cells is 12.2. You can modify the format for printing values in table cells by

- changing the default format with the FORMAT= option in the PROC TABULATE statement
- crossing elements in TABLE statement expressions with the F= format modifier.

The FORMAT= option, illustrated below, defines a default format for the entire table:

```
PROC TABULATE FORMAT=8.;
```

The F= format modifier is used in the TABLE statement to format the contents of selected cells. Format modifiers override the FORMAT= option in the PROC TABULATE statement, or the default format if no FORMAT= option is used. Format modifiers are described in more detail in the next section.

Note: the FORMAT statement and a format associated with the variable in the input data set have no effect on the contents of table cells. Formats associated with variables affect page, row, and column headings but not values in table cells. Refer to **PAGE, ROW, AND COLUMN HEADINGS** for more information on the use of the FORMAT statement.

Format Modifiers in TABLE Statement Expressions

The format modifier F= can be crossed with any variable or group of variables in the page, row, or column dimension of the TABLE statement. The format modifier defines formats for table cells at a more detailed level than the FORMAT= option of the PROC TABULATE statement.

Formatting an entire page of table cells

The location of the F= element in a TABLE statement determines how much of the table is affected by the format. If the F= element is used in the page dimension and no other format specifier appears in the TABLE statement, the values in all table cells on the page are formatted in the same manner. When the F= element is crossed with all elements in the page dimension, it produces the same effect as the FORMAT= option in the PROC TABULATE statement.†

For example, the following code creates a multipage table with all values in the table cells formatted using the 8.1 format:

```
PROC TABULATE DATA=DONORS;
    CLASS SEX BLDTYPE RHFACTOR;
    VAR HEMOGLOB;
    TABLE SEX*F=8.1,BLDTYPE,RHFACTOR*HEMOGLOB*MEAN;
RUN;
```

This code produces the two-page table illustrated in **Figure 5.23**.

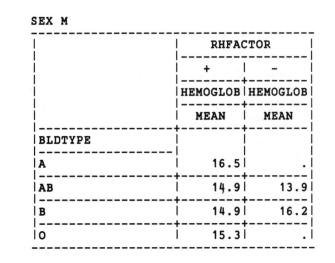

```
SEX F
-----------------------------------------
|               |       RHFACTOR        |
|               |-----------------------|
|               |    +     |    -       |
|               |----------+------------|
|               |HEMOGLOB  |HEMOGLOB    |
|               |----------+------------|
|               |  MEAN    |   MEAN     |
|---------------+----------+------------|
|BLDTYPE        |          |            |
|---------------|          |            |
|A              |    13.1  |     12.5   |
|---------------+----------+------------|
|B              |    15.6  |       .    |
|---------------+----------+------------|
|O              |    13.9  |     14.0   |
-----------------------------------------


SEX M
-----------------------------------------
|               |       RHFACTOR        |
|               |-----------------------|
|               |    +     |    -       |
|               |----------+------------|
|               |HEMOGLOB  |HEMOGLOB    |
|               |----------+------------|
|               |  MEAN    |   MEAN     |
|---------------+----------+------------|
|BLDTYPE        |          |            |
|---------------|          |            |
|A              |    16.5  |       .    |
|---------------+----------+------------|
|AB             |    14.9  |     13.9   |
|---------------+----------+------------|
|B              |    14.9  |     16.2   |
|---------------+----------+------------|
|O              |    15.3  |       .    |
-----------------------------------------
```

Figure 5.23   Formatting a Table with Multiple Pages

---

† If several elements are concatenated in the page dimension but only one of these elements is crossed with the format modifier, only the pages that involve that element are formatted according to the F= value.

Formatting selected rows of table cells

If the format modifier is used in the row dimension and no other format modifier appears in the column dimension, the values in all table cells in the affected rows are formatted in the same manner. For example, in **Figure 5.24** the table has rows for the HEMOGLOB averages in 4.1 format and the remaining rows in 4. format. Note that the F=4.1 element in the TABLE statement overrides the FORMAT=4. option in the PROC TABULATE statement for the first row of values only.

```
PROC TABULATE DATA=DONORS FORMAT=4. ;
   CLASS SEX BLDTYPE RHFACTOR;
   VAR HEMOGLOB;
   TABLE HEMOGLOB*MEAN*F=4.1 SEX,RHFACTOR*BLDTYPE;
RUN;
```

This code produces the following output.

		RHFACTOR							
		+				−			
		BLDTYPE				BLDTYPE			
		A	AB	B	O	A	AB	B	O
HEMOGLOB	MEAN	15.5	14.9	15.2	14.6	12.5	13.9	16.2	14.0
SEX									
F	N	3	.	1	5	1	.	.	2
M	N	7	1	1	5	.	1	1	.

Figure 5.24   Formatting Selected Rows of Table Cells

Formatting selected columns of table cells

If the format modifier is used in the column dimension, the values in all table cells in the affected columns are formatted in the same manner. For example, the following code creates a table with the columns for the HEMOGLOB averages in 8.1 format (as specified in the TABLE statement) and the remaining columns in 4. format (the default set up in the PROC TABULATE statement):

```
PROC TABULATE DATA=DONORS FORMAT=4. ;
   CLASS SEX BLDTYPE RHFACTOR;
   VAR HEMOGLOB;
   TABLE RHFACTOR*BLDTYPE,HEMOGLOB*MEAN*F=8.1 SEX;
RUN;
```

This code produces the output shown in **Figure 5.25**.

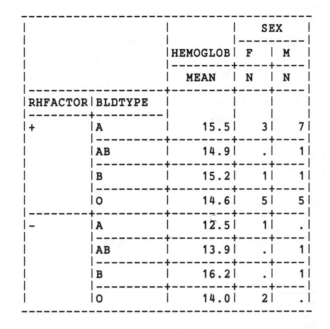

RHFACTOR	BLDTYPE	HEMOGLOB MEAN	SEX F N	M N
+	A	15.5	3	7
	AB	14.9	.	1
	B	15.2	1	1
	O	14.6	5	5
−	A	12.5	1	.
	AB	13.9	.	1
	B	16.2	.	1
	O	14.0	2	.

Figure 5.25   Formatting Selected Columns of Table Cells

Format modifiers in several dimensions

For many tables, you need a variety of formats to present your data in the most meaningful manner. You can use format modifiers on each dimension of a TABLE statement to achieve the results you need. In general, TABULATE uses the last format specified in a crossing to format the cells for that crossing. The actual order of precedence for formatting specifications is

- The FORMAT= option in the PROC TABULATE statement changes the default format. The default format and the format in the FORMAT= option are both overridden by a format modifier in the TABLE statement.
- Format modifiers used in the page dimension affect the values in all table cells on the page but are overridden by format modifiers in the column or row dimension.
- Format modifiers used in the row dimension affect the values in all table cells in the specified rows but are overridden by format modifiers in the column dimension.
- Format modifiers used in the column dimension affect the values in the table cells in the specified columns.

Controlling the Width of Columns

The widths of the columns in a PROC TABULATE table are determined by the largest format that can be printed in each column. In the simplest case, each dimension of the table is a single variable, and all values in the table cells have the same width, as in this TABLE statement:

```
TABLE A,X;
```

In most cases, the tables you print will be more complex than this simple example. The next few sections discuss how to print tables with more variables and differing formats.

Column widths of concatenated tables with the same formats

Chapter 4, "Learning to Use PROC TABULATE," discussed how TABLE statements can produce concatenated tables that are printed side by side or one after the other. The example below shows two concatenated tables (SEX, HEMOGLOB*MEAN and RHFACTOR,HEMOGLOB*MEAN) represented by Xs and Ys respectively. Because the format modifier is crossed with the column expression HEMOGLOB*MEAN, which is common to both tables, all cells have a width of 8.

```
PROC TABULATE DATA=DONORS;
    CLASS SEX BLDTYPE RHFACTOR;
    VAR HEMOGLOB;
    TABLE SEX RHFACTOR,HEMOGLOB*MEAN*F=8.1;
RUN;
```

Figure 5.26 illustrates the column widths produced by this code.

```
---------------------------------
|                   |HEMOGLOB|
|                   |--------|
|                   | MEAN   |
|-------------------+--------|
|SEX                |XXXXXXXX|
|-------------------|XXXXXXXX|
|F                  |XXXXXXXX|
|-------------------+XXXXXXXX|
|M                  |XXXXXXXX|
|-------------------+--------|
|RHFACTOR           |YYYYYYYY|
|-------------------|YYYYYYYY|
|+                  |YYYYYYYY|
|-------------------+YYYYYYYY|
|-                  |YYYYYYYY|
---------------------------------
```

Figure 5.26   Altering the Width of Cells in the Column Dimension

Similarly, when two concatenated tables share the same row definition, as in the example below, all columns are the same width.

```
TABLE HEMOGLOB*MEAN*F=8.1,SEX RHFACTOR;
```

This code produces output with columns widths like those in **Figure 5.27**.

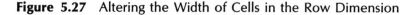

```
-----------------------------------------------------------------
|                 |        SEX        |      RHFACTOR     |
|                 |-------------------+------------------|
|                 |   F    |    M     |    +    |    -    |
|-----------------+--------+----------+---------+---------|
|HEMOGLOB|MEAN    |XXXXXXXX|XXXXXXXX|YYYYYYYY|YYYYYYYY|
-----------------------------------------------------------------
```

Figure 5.27   Altering the Width of Cells in the Row Dimension

Column widths of concatenated tables with different formats

Tables can have varying column widths in some situations. To illustrate when varying columns are possible, consider the general forms for concatenated tables with equal column widths, as illustrated in **Figure 5.28**.

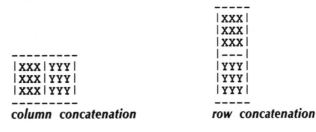

```
                                         -----
                                        |XXX|
                                        |XXX|
                                        |XXX|
             ---------                  |---|
            |XXX|YYY|                   |YYY|
            |XXX|YYY|                   |YYY|
            |XXX|YYY|                   |YYY|
             ---------                   -----
        column  concatenation        row  concatenation
```

Figure 5.28   Concatenated Tables

If the X table has a width of 3 and the Y table has a width of 6 and both tables are printed exactly according to the width of the format, the tables would look like those in **Figure 5.29**.

```
        --------------               -----
       |XXX|YYYYYY|                  |XXX|
       |XXX|YYYYYY|                  |XXX|
       |XXX|YYYYYY|                  |XXX|
        --------------               |-------|
                                     |YYYYYY|
                                     |YYYYYY|
                                     |YYYYYY|
                                      --------
```

Figure 5.29   Different Column Widths in Concatenated Tables

Obviously, the row concatenation in this figure does not have an acceptable column for a table. PROC TABULATE prints tables with varying column widths only when the tables are column concatenations, that is, when the tables are juxtaposed side by side.

The sample output in **Figure 5.30** has two concatenated tables, but the formats for the two tables are different. The first crossing (HEMOGLOB*MEAN,BLDTYPE) is formatted as 8.1, but the second table (SEX,BLDTYPE) defaults to the 4. format specified in the PROC TABULATE statement option. However, these tables are row concatenations, so a common column width must be used. The data printed in the cells are formatted differently for the two tables, but the width of all columns is 8 to accommodate the largest width.

```
PROC TABULATE DATA=DONORS FORMAT=4.;
   CLASS SEX BLDTYPE RHFACTOR;
   VAR HEMOGLOB;
   TABLE HEMOGLOB*MEAN* F=8.1 SEX,BLDTYPE;
RUN;
```

This code produces the following output.

```
-----------------------------------------------------------------
|              |        |              BLDTYPE               |
|              |        |-----------------------------------|
|              |        | A      | AB      | B      | O      |
|--------------+--------+--------+---------+--------+--------|
|HEMOGLOB|MEAN |        |XXXXXXXX|XXXXXXXX|XXXXXXXX|XXXXXXXX|
|--------+--------+--------+--------+---------+--------+--------|
|SEX     |        |        |  YYYY| YYYY|  YYYY|  YYYY|
|--------+--------------|        |  YYYY| YYYY|  YYYY|  YYYY|
|F       |N            |        |  YYYY| YYYY|  YYYY|  YYYY|
|--------+--------------+        |  YYYY| YYYY|  YYYY|  YYYY|
|M       |N            |        |  YYYY| YYYY|  YYYY|  YYYY|
-----------------------------------------------------------------
```

Figure 5.30   Different Cell Widths for Row Concatenations

When column concatenations have different format modifiers, the column widths can vary. In the following example, the first table, RHFACTOR*BLDTYPE, HEMOGLOB*MEAN is formatted with the 8.1 format; and the second table, RHFACTOR*BLDTYPE,SEX is formatted with the 4. format. Because the different formats do not need to share columns, as they do for the row concatenations in the preceding example, each table can have its own column width.

```
PROC TABULATE DATA=DONORS FORMAT=4.;
   CLASS SEX BLDTYPE RHFACTOR;
   VAR HEMOGLOB;
   TABLE RHFACTOR*BLDTYPE,HEMOGLOB*MEAN*F=8.1 SEX;
RUN;
```

Figure 5.31 illustrates the column widths produced by this code.

```
---------------------------------------------
|              |        |        |   SEX   |
|              |        |        |---------|
|              |        |HEMOGLOB| F  | M  |
|              |        |--------+----+----|
|              |        | MEAN   | N  | N  |
|--------------+--------+--------+----+----|
|RHFACTOR|BLDTYPE|XXXXXXXX|YYYY|YYYY|
|--------+--------- |XXXXXXXX|YYYY|YYYY|
|+       |A        |XXXXXXXX|YYYY|YYYY|
|        |--------+XXXXXXXX|YYYY|YYYY|
|        |AB       |XXXXXXXX|YYYY|YYYY|
|        |--------+XXXXXXXX|YYYY|YYYY|
|        |B        |XXXXXXXX|YYYY|YYYY|
|        |--------+XXXXXXXX|YYYY|YYYY|
|        |O        |XXXXXXXX|YYYY|YYYY|
|--------+--------+XXXXXXXX|YYYY|YYYY|
|-       |A        |XXXXXXXX|YYYY|YYYY|
|        |--------+XXXXXXXX|YYYY|YYYY|
|        |AB       |XXXXXXXX|YYYY|YYYY|
|        |--------+XXXXXXXX|YYYY|YYYY|
|        |B        |XXXXXXXX|YYYY|YYYY|
|        |--------+XXXXXXXX|YYYY|YYYY|
|        |O        |XXXXXXXX|YYYY|YYYY|
---------------------------------------------
```

Figure 5.31   Different Cell Widths for Column Concatenations

CHANGING TABLE OUTLINES

TABULATE provides several options to allow you to alter or remove the outlining characters for a table. This section discusses how to

- remove horizontal lines between rows
- remove all outlines
- redefine the characters used for outlining.

Removing Horizontal Lines

If you need to remove some of the horizontal lines generated by TABULATE for outlining parts of the table, use the NOSEPS option of the PROC TABULATE statement. This option removes only the horizontal lines between the rows in the body of the table.

The following code illustrates the effect of the NOSEPS option on a simple table. The first TABULATE step produces the default table with all of the horizontal lines. The second step produces the same table with the horizontal lines removed. This code

```
PROC TABULATE DATA=DONORS FORMAT=8.;
   CLASS BLDTYPE RHFACTOR;
   TABLE BLDTYPE,RHFACTOR;
PROC TABULATE DATA=DONORS FORMAT=8. NOSEPS;
   CLASS BLDTYPE RHFACTOR;
   TABLE BLDTYPE,RHFACTOR;
RUN;
```

produces the two tables shown in **Figure 5.32.†**

```
------------------------------------------------
|                      |      RHFACTOR          |
|                      |-----------------------|
|                      |   +    |    -          |
|                      |--------+--------------|
|                      |   N    |    N          |
|----------------------+--------+--------------|
|BLDTYPE               |        |               |
|----------------------|        |               |
|A                     |     10 |           1   |
|----------------------+--------+--------------|
|AB                    |      1 |           1   |
|----------------------+--------+--------------|
|B                     |      2 |           1   |
|----------------------+--------+--------------|
|O                     |     10 |           2   |
------------------------------------------------


------------------------------------------------
|                      |      RHFACTOR          |
|                      |-----------------------|
|                      |   +    |    -          |
|                      |--------+--------------|
|                      |   N    |    N          |
|----------------------+--------+--------------|
|BLDTYPE               |        |               |
|A                     |     10 |           1   |
|AB                    |      1 |           1   |
|B                     |      2 |           1   |
|O                     |     10 |           2   |
------------------------------------------------
```

Figure 5.32   Removing Horizontal Lines in Body of Table

---

† Compare the output in **Figure 5.32** to that in **Figure 5.33** to see how the NOSEPS option differs from setting the FORMCHAR= option to blanks.

Changing Outlining Characters

PROC TABULATE uses the FORMCHAR= values to produce the table outlines. The FORMCHAR= value is a string of 11 characters that define the

- vertical bar
- horizontal bar
- upper left intersection
- upper middle intersection
- upper right intersection
- middle left intersection
- middle middle (cross) intersection
- middle right intersection
- lower left intersection
- lower middle intersection
- lower right intersection.

The default values in the order listed above are FORMCHAR=' |---- | + |---'.

You can change the outlining characters with the SAS system option FORMCHAR= or the FORMCHAR= option in the PROC TABULATE statement. Use FORMCHAR='string' to change all the characters or a group of consecutive characters beginning with the first. Use FORMCHAR(n . . .)='string' to change only the characters at positions n. . . . For example,

```
FORMCHAR( 1  2)='XX'
```

changes the vertical and horizontal bars to X. The *string* value can be expressed as actual print characters (such as | and —) or as the hexadecimal equivalent for print characters (such as '4F'X).

If you use an IBM 6670 printer with an extended font (typestyle 27 or 225) with input character set 216, we recommend that you specify

```
FORMCHAR='FABFACCCBCEB8FECABCBBB'X
```

If you use an IBM 1403, 3211, or 3203-5 printer, or equivalent, with a TN (text) print train, we recommend that you specify

```
FORMCHAR='4FBFACBFBC4F8F4FABBFBB'X
```

Table 5.1 shows the characters produced by the default value and by the two suggested values. You can substitute any character or hexadecimal string for those given here to customize the appearance of the table.

Table 5.1 Characters Used with the FORMCHAR= Option

Name	Position	Default EBCDIC	ASCII	TN(text) print train	IBM 6670 printer with extended font
Vertical bar	1	|		|	|
		4F	7C	4F	FA
Horizontal bar	2	—		—	—
		60	2D	BF	BF
Upper left	3	—		⌈	⌈
		60	2D	AC	AC
Upper middle	4	—		—	⊤
		60	2D	BF	CC
Upper right	5	—		⌉	⌉
		60	2D	BC	BC
Middle left	6	|		|	⊢
		4F	7C	4F	EB
Middle middle	7	+		┼	┼
		4E	2B	8F	8F
Middle right	8	|		|	⊣
		4F	7C	4F	EC
Lower left	9	—		⌊	⌊
		60	2D	AB	AB
Lower middle	10	—		—	⊥
		60	2D	BF	CB
Lower right	11	—		⌋	⌋
		60	2D	BB	BB

You may prefer to remove all of the boxing characters from your output and insert only a few underlining characters in specific places. To do this, set all 11 characters of the FORMCHAR= option to blank and then assign headings in the TABLE statement to create the underlining for columns.† This technique is illustrated in this code:

```
PROC TABULATE DATA=DONORS FORMAT=3. FORMCHAR='            ';
    CLASS BLDTYPE RHFACTOR;
    TABLE BLDTYPE=' ',RHFACTOR='RH FACTOR'*N='---' / BOX=BLDTYPE;
RUN;
```

The output produced by these statements is illustrated in **Figure 5.33**.

BLDTYPE	RH FACTOR	
	+	-
	---	---
A	10	1
AB	1	1
B	2	1
O	10	2

Figure 5.33   Removing Outlining Characters with FORMCHAR= Option

The example in **Figure 5.34** illustrates the use of the FORMCHAR= option to replace the standard outlining characters with solid boxes. These statements

```
PROC TABULATE FORMCHAR='FABFACCCBCEB8FECABCBBB'X
    DATA=DONORS FORMAT=8.;
    CLASS SEX;
    VAR HEMOGLOB;
    TABLE SEX,HEMOGLOB*MEAN;
RUN;
```

produce the boxing characters illustrated in **Figure 5.34**.

	HEMOGLOB
	MEAN
SEX	
F	14
M	16

Figure 5.34   Altering Table Outlines

---

† Compare the output in **Figure 5.32** to that in **Figure 5.33** to see how the NOSEPS option differs from setting the FORMCHAR= option to blanks. Note that the column widths are narrower and the BOX= option is used in **Figure 5.33** to improve the appearance of a table without vertical bars.

SAMPLE APPLICATIONS

Public Health Clinic Example

A Multiple-Response Example

Chapter 6
Public Health
Clinic Example

The sample application presented in this chapter uses a public health clinic as a context for illustrating uses of PROC TABULATE. Although this chapter focuses on a single industry, the coding techniques shown here are widely applicable and illustrate the interaction of many features of the TABULATE procedure.

Recommended Use

All users: refer to this chapter for illustrations of techniques described in the rest of the book, and study the DATA steps for examples of how you can reshape data.

Contents

PURPOSE OF THE EXAMPLE

A public health clinic collects information on each visit by a patient. From this information, the clinic can study the services they provide, the types of illness they encounter, the activity of their health care professionals, and the worth and income generated by their service.

Some of the reports a clinic might want to generate are

- financial reports that compare worth of services to actual income
- reports that show the activity of each group of health care professionals
- epidemiology reports that list all infectious diseases encountered within a month and year-to-date
- studies of activity in the clinic for each weekday.

This section illustrates these applications. From these applications, you can see examples of how to use the following techniques with PROC TABULATE:

- obtaining percentages of column totals as well as other totals
- tailoring column widths individually for specific types of information
- crossing multiple variables in one dimension of the table
- varying the order of the headings by specifying the ORDER= option
- sorting data when the ORDER= option does not produce the desired results
- printing column and row totals by specifying the ALL class variable
- limiting the scope of the ALL class variable
- creating a class variable with seven values (the days of the week) and then analyzing a year of data by weekday activity.

The Data

The data set used in this study contains relatively standard information gathered on patients as they visit health clinics. The data set contains 1498 observations, which represent a year of activity at a clinic.

The output from PROC CONTENTS, illustrated in **Output 6.1**, describes the data set used in this study. Following the PROC CONTENTS listing is a brief description of each of the variables in the data set. The PROC PRINT listing in **Output 6.2** illustrates the first 40 observations in the data set.

Output 6.1   Contents of CLINIC Data Set

```
                        CONTENTS PROCEDURE
                  CONTENTS OF SAS MEMBER IN.CLINIC

CREATED BY OS JOB CREATE    ON CPUID 12-3456-789000
AT 15:43 THURSDAY, FEBRUARY 5, 1987   BY SAS RELEASE 5.16
DSNAME=SASABC.MISC.SASDATA   OBSERVATIONS PER TRACK =460   BLKSIZE=23464
LRECL=102   GENERATED BY DATA
NUMBER OF OBSERVATIONS: 1498   NUMBER OF VARIABLES: 24
MEMTYPE:   DATA

            ----ALPHABETIC LIST OF VARIABLES AND ATTRIBUTES-----
    # VARIABLE TYPE   LENGTH POSITION FORMAT      INFORMAT     LABEL
   22 AGE      NUM       8      78
   21 BILLPCNT NUM       8      70
   19 BRTHDATE NUM       8      54 DATE7.
```

(continued on next page)

(continued from previous page)

```
 5 DIAG1     CHAR    4      21
 6 DIAG2     CHAR    4      25
 7 DIAG3     CHAR    4      29
 1 PATIENT   NUM     8       4
 3 PROV1     CHAR    4      13
 4 PROV2     CHAR    4      17
 8 SERV1     CHAR    2      33
 9 SERV2     CHAR    2      35
10 SERV3     CHAR    2      37
11 SERV4     CHAR    2      39
12 SERV5     CHAR    2      41
13 SERV6     CHAR    2      43
14 SERV7     CHAR    2      45
15 SERV8     CHAR    2      47
16 SERV9     CHAR    2      49
17 SERV10    CHAR    2      51
18 SEX       CHAR    1      53
 2 SITE      CHAR    1      12
23 TOTBILL   NUM     8      86
24 TOTDUE    NUM     8      94
20 VISTDATE  NUM     8      62 DATE7.
```

AGE	is calculated from the VISTDATE minus the BRTHDATE.
BILLPCNT	is a number indicating the percentage of the bill that the patient can pay.
BRTHDATE	is the date of birth in DATE7. format.
DIAG1 DIAG2 DIAG3	are codes indicating the diagnoses.
PATIENT	is a number identifying the patient.
PROV1 PROV2	are codes indicating who provided services.
SERV1 through SERV10	are codes indicating the type of services provided to the patient.
SEX	is a 1-character code for male or female.
SITE	is the location of the clinic where services are performed.
TOTBILL	is the total value of all services provided at this visit.
TOTDUE	is the amount of the total bill that the patient is expected to pay. This value is calculated by multiplying TOTBILL by BILLPCNT.
VISTDATE	is the date that the patient was seen in DATE7. format.

Output 6.2 shows a small portion of the data used in this example.

Output 6.2   Sample Observations from CLINIC Data Set

```
                                                                                            1

      P                                                               B    V   B
      A                                                               R    I   I
      T                                                               T    S   L
      I         P    P    D    D  D  S  S  S  S  S  S  S S S S         H    T   L        T
      E    S    R    R    I    I  I  E  E  E  E  E  E  E E E E  S      D    D   L        O   T
   O  N    I    O    O    A    A  E  R  R  R  R  R  R  R R R R  E      A    A   P  A  B   T   O
   B  T    T    V    V    G    G  G  V  V  V  V  V  V  V V V V  X      T    T   C  G  I   B   T
   S  E    E    1    2    1    2  3  1  2  3  4  5  6  7 8 9 0         E    E   N  E  L   I   D
                                                                                 T          L   U  E

   1  15421 S 1601      401      AA CJ             F 22JUL24 27JAN86  80 61 31 24.8
   2  15421 S 1601      3000     AA CB CJ          F 22JUL24 22MAR86  99 61 46 46.0
   3  15422 S 1003      466      AB CM             F 15NOV66 06JAN86  60 19 38 22.8
   4  15422 S 1004      460      AA                F 15NOV66 08MAY86  99 19 16 16.0
   5  15422 P 1606      6264     AA                F 15NOV66 26MAR86  40 19 16  6.4
   6  15422 S 1003      3000     AA                F 15NOV66 30JAN86  20 19 16  3.2
   7  15422 S 1003      713  712 AA                F 15NOV66 17JAN86  40 19 16  6.4
   8  15432 S 1601      345      AA                F 29APR53 17JUL86  99 33 16 16.0
   9  15442 S 1004      7805     AA                F 21DEC33 29MAY86  20 52 16  3.2
  10  15442 S 1003      7805     AB                F 21DEC33 20MAR86  20 52 23  4.6
  11  15442 S 9006      7805     AA                F 21DEC33 23AUG86  20 52 16  3.2
  12  15442 S 1004      7805     AA                F 21DEC33 10AUG86  20 52 16  3.2
  13  15442 S 1004      7805     AA                F 21DEC33 08AUG86  20 52 16  3.2
  14  15442 S 1601      460      AA                F 21DEC33 05OCT86  99 52 16 16.0
  15  15451 S 1607      034  460 AB ZZ             F 16MAY43 09JUN86  99 43 38 38.0
  16  15451 S 1601      009      AB CA CJ          F 16MAY43 26SEP86  99 43 53 53.0
  17  15453 S 1551      034  463 AC CA CJ CM CS ZZ M 16APR80 14MAY86  99  6 105 105.0
  18  15453 S 1551      463      AB CM             M 16APR80 28FEB86  99  5 38 38.0
  19  15453 S 1603      3810     AA CM             M 16APR80 09FEB86   0  5 31  0.0
  20  15481 S 1607 3011 466  460 AB                F 06FEB42 21JUL86  99 44 23 23.0
  21  15481 S 1009      460      AB CM             F 06FEB42 19JUL86  99 44 38 38.0
  22  15482 S 1606      691      AB                M 05OCT66 03FEB86  99 19 23 23.0
  23  15484 S 1601      507      AD ML CB CJ       M 01AUG71 12JUN86  99 14 78 78.0
  24  15484 S 1003      691      AB                M 01AUG71 18JUN86  99 14 23 23.0
  25  15485 S 1606      280      AB CB             F 18JAN82 26JUN86  99  4 38 38.0
  26  15501 S 1003      401      AA                M 19JAN58 13AUG86  20 28 16  3.2
  27  15502 S 1606      692      AB                F 06JUL53 26MAY86  99 32 23 23.0
  28  15503 S 1004      7960     AA FK             F 14SEP65 16MAR86  99 20 31 31.0
  29  15503 A 1605      7874     AB                F 14SEP65 15MAR86  99 20 23 23.0
  30  15504 S 1601      493      AB                M 26DEC72 12SEP86  99 13 23 23.0
  31  15504 S 1010      493  507 AC                M 26DEC72 18SEP86  99 13 30 30.0
  32  15504 S 1010      493  507 AC                M 26DEC72 25SEP86  99 13 30 30.0
  33  15504 S 1004      685      AB                M 26DEC72 16NOV86  99 13 23 23.0
  34  15505 S 1601      7830     AB                M 14MAY74 18SEP86  99 12 23 23.0
  35  15505 S 1010      493  507 AC                M 14MAY74 25SEP86  99 12 30 30.0
  36  15506 S 1551      466      AB                F 17JUN83 01FEB86  99  2 23 23.0
  37  15506 S 1601      460      AB CM             F 17JUN83 23MAR86  99  2 38 38.0
  38  15506 S 1004      466      AA CN             F 17JUN83 23MAR86  99  2 31 31.0
  39  15506 S 1601      889      AB                F 17JUN83 21SEP86  99  3 23 23.0
  40  15506 S 1551      464      AB CM             F 17JUN83 22OCT86  99  3 38 38.0
```

Formatting the Data

Some of the variables in this data set are more useful when they are formatted. The PROC FORMAT coding below creates the formats used in the rest of this section:

```
PROC FORMAT;
   VALUE $SITE
      'S'='Main Clinic'
      'A'='Adolescent Center'
      OTHER='Other sites';
   VALUE $PROVIDE
      '1000'-'1099'='MD '
      '1300'-'1499'='MD - Specialist '
      '1500'-'1599'='MD - Child Specialist'
      '1600'-'1699'='Nurse Practitioner'
      '3000'-'3199','3301'='Nurse '
      '3200'-'3269'='Counselor '
      '3270'-'3299'='Podiatrist '
      '4000'-'4999'='Nutritionist'
```

```
                '5000'-'6005'='Technician'
                '6006'-'6999'='Eye Specialist'
                '9000'-'9999'='MD - Referred Out';
          VALUE $DIAGINF
                '008'='Intestinal infection'
                '009'='Infectious colitus'
                '0091'='Infectious enteritis'
                '011'='Pulmonary TB'
                '033'='Whooping cough'
                '034'='Strep throat'
                '052'='Chicken pox'
                '053'='Herpes zoster'
                '054'='Herpes simplex'
                '070'='Viral hepatitis'
                '072'='Mumps'
                '075'='Infectious mononucleosis'
                '078'='Other virus'
                '0791'='Echo virus'
                '0799'='Unknown virus'
                '084'='Malaria'
                '090'='Congenital syphilis'
                '098'='Gonococcal infection'
                '110'='Dermatophytosis'
                '112'='Candidiasis'
                '1121'='Genital candidiasis'
                '127'='Intestinal worm'
                '131'='Trichomoniasis'
                '132'='Lice'
                '133'='Scabies'
                '136'='Other parasitic disease'
                '460'='Common cold'
                '461' - '4619'='Sinusitis'
                '462'='Pharyngitis'
                '480' - '486'='Pneumonia'
                '487' - '4879'='Influenza'
                other='(Non-infectious)';
          VALUE DAYFORM
                1='Sunday'
                2='Monday'
                3='Tuesday'
                4='Wednesday'
                5='Thursday'
                6='Friday'
                7='Saturday';
          RUN;
```

EXAMPLE 1: REPORTING ON WORTH OF SERVICES VERSUS INCOME

This example illustrates a financial report that compares the worth of services provided by each group of health care professionals to the actual income for those services. As a provider of public health care, this clinic charges only the amount that a patient can afford for services. This value is calculated and stored in TOTDUE. The clinic also records the full value of the services they provide in the TOTBILL variable. By using the PCTSUM statistic, they can compare the sum of total worth of services to the total of the billed amounts.

A secondary purpose for this report is to show the activity of each group of health care professionals at the clinic. The report focuses on the primary provider of services, PROV1. For each group of health care professionals, the table reports

- the total number of visits handled by a group
- the average worth of the services for a visit
- the total worth of services provided by the group
- the percentage of each group's activity to the total activity for the clinic.

The code used to generate this table is shown below. For more information on the input data set and user-written formats used in this code, refer to **Formatting the Data**. The circled numbers to the left of the code indicate important coding techniques that are discussed in detail following the code. The output from this code is shown in **Output 6.3**.

```
PROC TABULATE DATA=IN.CLINIC MISSING FORMAT=10.2;
❶   FORMAT SITE $SITE. PROV1 $PROVIDE.;
    CLASS SITE PROV1;
    VAR TOTBILL TOTDUE;
    TABLE SITE='Clinic location' ALL='All clinics',
❷        (PROV1=' ' ALL='Summary')*
❸        (N='# of visits'*F=6. TOTBILL='Worth of Services'*(MEAN SUM
❹        PCTSUM<SITE*PROV1*TOTBILL
                SITE*ALL*TOTBILL
                ALL*PROV1*TOTBILL
                ALL*TOTBILL>='% of worth to worth of all services')
❺        TOTDUE='Amount Billed'*
❻        (SUM PCTSUM<TOTBILL>='% of worth'*F=7.2)) / RTS=12 CONDENSE;
    KEYLABEL SUM='Total' MEAN='Average';
RUN;
```

1. Both of these formats are user-written. The first one, $SITE., provides descriptive labels to the codes for SITE. The second format, $PROVIDE., actually establishes the classes for the class variable, PROV1. Refer to **Formatting the Data** for the complete listing of these user-written formats.
2. By placing the ALL class variable in a parenthetical group, you limit its scope to only the variables within the group. Although the TOTDUE variable occurs in the same dimension of the table, it is not affected by the ALL variable because it is not within the parentheses. Note also that the heading for PROV1 is blanked out to remove some of the multiple levels of headings that occur when several class variables are crossed in the same dimension.
3. The format modifier for N (F=6.) tailors the width of the column and the format of the values in the table cells in this column to a more appropriate format for the type of data being printed.
4. This TABLE statement requests that two types of percentages be calculated. The first one compares the sum in a single table cell of the TOTBILL column (the Total column under Worth of Services) to the total worth of services for all providers at all clinics (obtained by summing the values in all TOTBILL cells). Note that the denominator definition has four expressions concatenated within it. All four of these expressions are necessary to provide a denominator for all possible crossings. The order of denominators may be important. If you specify two denominators that

can be used for a single crossing, TABULATE uses the first one it encounters to calculate the percentage.

5. The second percentage calculated for this table compares the sum in each TOTDUE cell (the Total column under Amount Billed) to the corresponding sum in the TOTBILL cell. Because there are no class variables in this denominator definition, the same denominator can be used for values in single cells and column totals.

6. The CONDENSE option is used to print several logical pages on one physical page. This is particularly useful for tables that are short and wide.

Output 6.3 Worth of Service versus Income

1

| | | MD | | | | | MD - Specialist | | | | |
| | | Worth of Services | | | Amount Billed | | | Worth of Services | | | Amount Billed | |
	# of visits	Average	Total	% of worth to worth of all services	Total	% of worth	# of visits	Average	Total	% of worth to worth of all services	Total	% of worth
Clinic location												
Adolescent Center	1	30.00	30.00	0.06	30.00	100.00	.	.	.	.	.	.
Other sites	20	27.10	542.00	1.12	366.80	67.68	.	.	.	.	.	.
Main Clinic	813	30.82	25056.00	51.71	18697.20	74.62	6	48.33	290.00	0.60	277.00	95.52
All clinics	834	30.73	25628.00	52.89	19094.00	74.50	6	48.33	290.00	0.60	277.00	95.52

(CONTINUED)

| | | MD - Child Specialist | | | | | Nurse Practitioner | | | | | |
| | | Worth of Services | | | Amount Billed | | | Worth of Services | | | Amount Billed | |
	# of visits	Average	Total	% of worth to worth of all services	Total	% of worth	# of visits	Average	Total	% of worth to worth of all services	Total	% of worth
Clinic location												
Adolescent Center	.	.	.	.	.	.	17	37.53	638.00	1.32	638.00	100.00
Other sites	.	.	.	.	.	.	42	24.38	1024.00	2.11	844.00	82.42
Main Clinic	74	33.09	2449.00	5.05	1841.20	75.18	341	31.83	10853.00	22.40	8363.10	77.06
All clinics	74	33.09	2449.00	5.05	1841.20	75.18	400	31.29	12515.00	25.83	9845.10	78.67

(CONTINUED)

2

| | | Nurse | | | | | | | Counselor | | | | |
| | | Worth of Services | | | Amount Billed | | | | Worth of Services | | | Amount Billed | |
	# of visits	Average	Total	% of worth to worth of all services	Total	% of worth	# of visits	Average	Total	% of worth to worth of all services	Total	% of worth
Clinic location												
Adolescent Center	.	.	.	.	.	.	11	75.09	826.00	1.70	826.00	100.00
Other sites	.	.	.	.	.	.	1	80.00	80.00	0.17	80.00	100.00
Main Clinic	66	30.64	2022.00	4.17	1653.00	81.75	52	61.58	3202.00	6.61	2143.00	66.93
All clinics	66	30.64	2022.00	4.17	1653.00	81.75	64	64.19	4108.00	8.48	3049.00	74.22

(CONTINUED)

| | | Podiatrist | | | | | | | Technician | | | | |
| | | Worth of Services | | | Amount Billed | | | | Worth of Services | | | Amount Billed | |
	# of visits	Average	Total	% of worth to worth of all services	Total	% of worth	# of visits	Average	Total	% of worth to worth of all services	Total	% of worth
Clinic location												
Adolescent Center	.	.	.	.	.	.	.	.	.	.	.	.
Other sites	.	.	.	.	.	.	.	.	.	.	.	.
Main Clinic	35	31.51	1103.00	2.28	932.20	84.51	5	18.80	94.00	0.19	94.00	100.00
All clinics	35	31.51	1103.00	2.28	932.20	84.51	5	18.80	94.00	0.19	94.00	100.00

(CONTINUED)

| | | Eye Specialist | | | | | MD – Referred Out | | | | | |
| | | Worth of Services | | | Amount Billed | | | Worth of Services | | | Amount Billed | |
	# of visits	Average	Total	% of worth to worth of all services	Total	% of worth	# of visits	Average	Total	% of worth to worth of all services	Total	% of worth
Clinic location												
Adolescent Center	.	.	.	.	.	.	.	.	.	.	.	.
Other sites	.	.	.	.	.	.	.	.	.	.	.	.
Main Clinic	4	16.00	64.00	0.13	48.00	75.00	10	18.10	181.00	0.37	88.80	49.06
All clinics	4	16.00	64.00	0.13	48.00	75.00	10	18.10	181.00	0.37	88.80	49.06

(CONTINUED)

| | | Summary | | | | |
| | | Worth of Services | | | Amount Billed | |
	# of visits	Average	Total	% of worth to worth of all services	Total	% of worth
Clinic location						
Adolescent Center	29	51.52	1494.00	3.08	1494.00	100.00
Other sites	63	26.13	1646.00	3.40	1290.80	78.42
Main Clinic	1406	32.23	45314.00	93.52	34137.50	75.34
All clinics	1498	32.35	48454.00	100.00	36922.30	76.20

EXAMPLE 2: REFORMATTING THE OUTPUT

The table produced in this example contains exactly the same information as that in example 1. The format of the column headings for this table differ, however. This example illustrates how minor changes to the code can alter the appearance of the table.

   The code used to generate this table is shown below. For more information on the input data set and user-written formats used in this code, refer to **Formatting the Data**. The circled numbers to the left of the code indicate important coding techniques that are discussed in detail following the code. The first page of output from this code is shown in **Output 6.4**. A single page of output is sufficient for comparison to **Output 6.3**.

```
PROC TABULATE DATA=IN.CLINIC MISSING FORMAT=10.2;
    CLASS SITE PROV1;
    FORMAT SITE $SITE. PROV1 $PROVIDE.;
    VAR TOTBILL TOTDUE;
    TABLE SITE='Clinic location' ALL='All clinics',
         (PROV1=' ' ALL='Summary')*
❶       (N='# of visits'*F=6. TOTBILL=' '*
         (MEAN='Average worth of services' SUM='Total worth of services'
         PCTSUM<SITE*PROV1*TOTBILL
               SITE*ALL*TOTBILL
               ALL*PROV1*TOTBILL
               ALL*TOTBILL>='% of worth to worth of all services')
❷       TOTDUE=' '*(SUM='Total amount billed'
         PCTSUM<TOTBILL>='% of billed to worth'*F=7.2))
         / RTS=12 CONDENSE;
RUN;
```

1. By blanking out the heading for TOTBILL and TOTDUE, the number of column headings is reduced and their appearance is more uniform.
2. To ensure that the column headings are uniform, you have to remove excess headings from all of the concatenated variables in the column dimension.

Output 6.4 Reformatted Worth of Services versus Income

		MD						**MD – Specialist**				
	# of visits	Average worth of services	Total worth of services	% of worth to worth of all services	Total amount billed	% of billed to worth	# of visits	Average worth of services	Total worth of services	% of worth to worth of all services	Total amount billed	% of billed to worth
Clinic location												
Adolescent Center	1	30.00	30.00	0.06	30.00	100.00	.	.	.	.	.	.
Other sites	20	27.10	542.00	1.12	366.80	67.68	.	.	.	.	.	.
Main Clinic	813	30.82	25056.00	51.71	18697.20	74.62	6	48.33	290.00	0.60	277.00	95.52
All clinics	834	30.73	25628.00	52.89	19094.00	74.50	6	48.33	290.00	0.60	277.00	95.52

(CONTINUED)

(continued on next page)

(continued from previous page)

		MD – Child Specialist					Nurse Practitioner				
	# of visits	Average worth of services	Total worth of services	% of worth to worth of all services	Total amount billed	% of billed to worth	# of visits	Average worth of services	Total worth of services	% of worth to worth of all services	Total amount billed	% of billed to worth
Clinic location												
Adolescent Center	.	.	.	.	.	.	17	37.53	638.00	1.32	638.00	100.00
Other sites	.	.	.	.	.	.	42	24.38	1024.00	2.11	844.00	82.42
Main Clinic	74	33.09	2449.00	5.05	1841.20	75.18	341	31.83	10853.00	22.40	8363.10	77.06
All clinics	74	33.09	2449.00	5.05	1841.20	75.18	400	31.29	12515.00	25.83	9845.10	78.67

EXAMPLE 3: REPORTING INFECTIOUS DISEASES

This example illustrates how you can reshape the data in your original data set and then use TABULATE to report on the newly created data set. In this example, the clinic needs to analyze all diagnoses recorded within a month to track what infectious diseases have occurred. The problem with the original data set is that each observation has up to three diagnoses (DIAG1 through DIAG3). To treat all diagnoses as one variable, the clinic restructures the data by producing a separate observation for each diagnosis and storing the diagnosis in a new variable DIAG.

As for the PROV1 variable used in examples 1 and 2, the DIAG variable has to be formatted to create manageable classes. In this case, however, it would improve the appearance of the table to print the DIAG values by their formatted order. Thus, this example uses the ORDER=FORMATTED option in the PROC TABULATE statement.

Note that the first formatted value printed in the table is actually the OTHER class set up in the PROC FORMAT step in **Formatting the Data**. By enclosing this formatted value in parentheses, you can force the OTHER class to print first and not be embedded alphabetically in the middle of the other classes.

The code used to generate this table is shown below. For more information on the input data set and user-written formats used in this code, refer to **Formatting the Data**. The circled numbers to the left of the code indicate important coding techniques that are discussed in detail following the code. The output from this code is shown in **Output 6.5**.

```
     DATA TEMP;
        SET IN.CLINIC;
        KEEP DIAG SITE VISTDATE;
❶      IF '01DEC86'D <= VISTDATE <= '31DEC86'D THEN DO;
❷         IF DIAG1 THEN DO;
             DIAG=DIAG1;
             OUTPUT;
          END;
```

```
         IF DIAG2 THEN DO;
            DIAG=DIAG2;
            OUTPUT;
            END;
         IF DIAG3 THEN DO;
            DIAG=DIAG3;
            OUTPUT;
            END;
         END;
❸ PROC TABULATE DATA=TEMP FORMAT=6. MISSING ORDER=FORMATTED;
      CLASS SITE DIAG VISTDATE;
❹    FORMAT VISTDATE DDMMYY2. SITE   $SITE. DIAG $DIAGINF.;
❺    TABLE SITE='Infectious Diseases at',
            DIAG='DIAGNOSIS',
            VISTDATE='DAY OF THE MONTH'*N=' '
❻          / RTS=14 BOX='December' PRINTMISS;
   RUN;
```

1. The first table reports the visits that occurred in a single month, so a DATA step is required to select only those observations. If the SAS macro facility is available at your site, you may want to use it to simplify the changes that regularly need to be made to the code.
2. This DATA step creates a temporary file that has separate observations for each diagnosis in the original observation. Creating this new data set allows you to study all diagnoses as a single class variable.
3. Using the ORDER=FORMATTED option allows you to organize the two principal variables in the table: DIAG and VISTDATE. The formatted diagnoses appear in alphabetical order, and the formatted dates appear in numerical order.
4. This FORMAT statement specifies the SAS date format DDMMYY2. so that only the day is printed. The remainder of the formats are user-written. Refer to **Formatting the Data** for descriptions of these formats.
5. The heading assigned to replace the SITE heading makes use of the values that are also printed for the class variable, SITE.
6. The BOX= option names the month reported in the table. Like the values in the DATA step described in 1 above, this value needs to vary each time the report is generated. The PRINTMISS option is used to ensure that all pages of the report are treated uniformly. Note that values that do not occur in the data set, such as December 6, do not print even when you specify PRINTMISS.

Output 6.5   Infectious Diseases

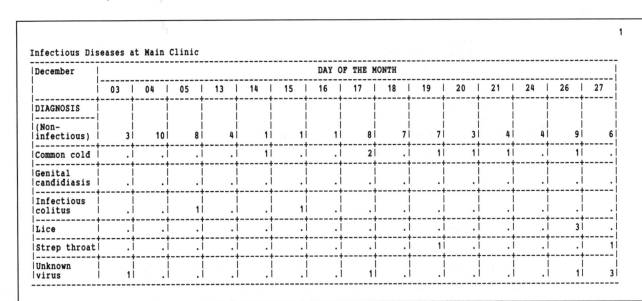

Infectious Diseases at Main Clinic

December	DAY OF THE MONTH														
	03	04	05	13	14	15	16	17	18	19	20	21	24	26	27
DIAGNOSIS															
(Non-infectious)	3	10	8	4	1	1	1	8	7	7	3	4	4	9	6
Common cold	.	.	.	.	1	.	.	2	.	1	1	1	.	1	.
Genital candidiasis	.	.	.	.	.	.	.	.	.	.	.	.	.	.	.
Infectious colitus	.	.	1	.	.	1	.	.	.	.	.	.	.	.	.
Lice	.	.	.	.	.	.	.	.	.	.	.	.	.	3	.
Strep throat	.	.	.	.	.	.	.	.	.	1	.	.	.	.	1
Unknown virus	1	.	.	.	.	.	.	1	.	.	.	.	.	1	3

1

Infectious Diseases at Other sites

December	DAY OF THE MONTH														
	03	04	05	13	14	15	16	17	18	19	20	21	24	26	27
DIAGNOSIS															
(Non-infectious)	.	1	.	.	.	.	.	.	.	.	.	.	.	.	.
Common cold	.	.	.	.	.	.	.	.	.	.	.	.	.	.	.
Genital candidiasis	.	.	.	.	1	.	.	.	.	.	.	.	.	.	.
Infectious colitus	.	.	.	.	1	.	.	.	.	.	.	.	.	.	.
Lice	.	.	.	.	.	.	.	.	.	.	.	.	.	.	.
Strep throat	.	.	.	.	.	.	.	.	.	.	.	.	.	.	.
Unknown virus	.	.	.	.	.	.	.	.	.	.	.	.	.	.	.

2

EXAMPLE 4: YEAR-TO-DATE REPORTING

This example is similar to example 3 in that it uses the same data set and formatting techniques for diagnoses. In addition to the difficulties encountered in example 3, this example also has to solve the problem of how to print a table when some values need to be in formatted order and some need to be in the order of the actual values of the class variables.

The solution in this case is to use PROC SORT to order the data and then specify the ORDER=DATA option in the PROC TABULATE statement. Please keep in mind, however, that this technique does not always produce the desired results.†
For ORDER=DATA to produce both headings in sorted order, all values of the second variable must occur for the first value of the first variable. The first value of FORMDIAG in this example satisfies this condition. That is, the OTHER category has observations for each month of the year, so the months are sorted correctly.

The code used to generate the table shown in **Output 6.6** is shown below. For more information on the input data set and user-written formats used in this code, refer to **Formatting the Data**. The circled numbers to the left of the code indicate important coding techniques that are discussed in detail following the code.

```
❶  DATA TEMP;
       SET IN.CLINIC;
       KEEP FORMDIAG VISTDATE SITE;
       IF DIAG1 THEN DO;
❷          FORMDIAG=PUT(DIAG1,$DIAGINF.);
           OUTPUT;
           END;
       IF DIAG2 THEN DO;
           FORMDIAG=PUT(DIAG2,$DIAGINF.);
           OUTPUT;
           END;
       IF DIAG3 THEN DO;
           FORMDIAG=PUT(DIAG3,$DIAGINF.);
           OUTPUT;
           END;
   PROC SORT DATA=TEMP;
❸     BY FORMDIAG VISTDATE;
❹  PROC TABULATE DATA=TEMP FORMAT=7. MISSING ORDER=DATA;
       CLASS SITE FORMDIAG VISTDATE;
       FORMAT VISTDATE MONYY5. SITE  $SITE.;
       TABLE SITE='Infectious Diseases at',
             FORMDIAG='DIAGNOSIS',
             VISTDATE='MONTHLY TOTALS'*N=' '
             ALL='TOTAL TO DATE'*N=' '*F=5.
❺           / RTS=18 BOX='Year-to-date';
   RUN;
```

1. The purpose of the DATA and PROC SORT steps is to allow one variable (DIAG) to be ordered by its formatted value (stored in the new variable FORMDIAG) and a second variable (VISTDATE) to be ordered by its actual value. This problem was not an issue in the previous report because only the day value of the date was used. When the date is expressed with the MONYY5. format and it is printed in order of its formatted value, APR86 is printed before JAN86.
2. The PUT function is used to create a new variable that has a formatted value. For example, if the value of the DIAG variable is 008, the value of FORMDIAG is Intestinal infection, which is determined by the $DIAGINF. format. Refer to **Formatting the Data** for a complete description of the $DIAGINF. format.

---

† Refer to **Why Are the Headings in This Order** in Appendix 2 for an illustration of when this technique does not work.

3. The BY statement in the PROC SORT step indicates that you want to sort all values of VISTDATE within each value of FORMDIAG, the variable produced in the preceding DATA step. In this case, the first value of FORMDIAG is the largest group of observations, and all values of VISTDATE occur within the first value of FORMDIAG. It is important to note that this technique works only in this situation: when all values of the second variable occur for the first value of the first variable. Refer to **Why Are the Headings in This Order** in Appendix 2, "Answers to Common Questions," for a more detailed explanation.
4. The final step to ensuring that the table is ordered as you want it to be is to specify the ORDER=DATA option. This tells TABULATE to use the sorted order produced by PROC SORT. If you omit this option, the DATA step and PROC SORT step have no effect on the output because TABULATE defaults to ORDER=INTERNAL.
5. Note that this TABLE statement does not specify the PRINTMISS option, so the output has varying column and row headings for each page of the table. If the PRINTMISS option were added, the output from this code would have the same row and column headings on each page, as shown in **Output 6.5**.

Output 6.6   Year-to-Date Report of Infectious Diseases

1

Infectious Diseases at Main Clinic

Year-to-date	MONTHLY TOTALS												TOTAL TO DATE
	JAN86	FEB86	MAR86	APR86	MAY86	JUN86	JUL86	AUG86	SEP86	OCT86	NOV86	DEC86	
DIAGNOSIS													
(Non-infectious)	131	119	150	120	130	128	68	145	96	128	82	76	1373
Candidiasis	1	.	.	.	.	.	.	.	.	.	.	.	1
Chicken pox	2	.	3	6	.	.	.	1	.	.	.	.	12
Common cold	14	2	16	13	6	4	7	4	7	11	9	7	100
Congenital syphilis	.	.	.	.	.	.	1	.	1	.	.	.	2
Dermatophytosis	.	.	1	.	.	.	.	3	.	.	.	.	4
Echo virus	2	1	.	.	.	1	.	1	.	1	1	.	7
Herpes simplex	.	.	.	.	.	.	1	.	1	.	.	.	2
Herpes zoster	.	.	.	.	.	.	.	1	.	.	.	.	1
Infectious colitus	.	.	1	.	.	.	.	1	2	3	1	2	10
Infectious enteritis	1	.	.	.	1	.	1	2	1	.	.	.	6
Infectious mononucleosis	1	.	.	.	.	.	.	.	.	.	.	.	1
Lice	.	.	1	1	.	.	.	.	1	.	.	3	6
Malaria	.	1	.	.	.	.	.	.	.	.	.	.	1
Other virus	3	.	.	4	1	.	.	.	1	.	.	.	9

(continued on next page)

(continued from previous page)

	JAN	FEB	MAR	APR	MAY	JUN	JUL	AUG	SEP	OCT	NOV	DEC	TOTAL
Pneumonia	.	1	.	2	1	.	.	1	.	.	.	.	5
Pulmonary TB	8	2	2	3	5	.	.	2	1	.	1	.	24
Scabies	.	.	.	1	.	1	.	.	.	.	.	.	2

(CONTINUED)

2

Infectious Diseases at Main Clinic

Year-to-date	MONTHLY TOTALS												TOTAL TO DATE
	JAN86	FEB86	MAR86	APR86	MAY86	JUN86	JUL86	AUG86	SEP86	OCT86	NOV86	DEC86	
DIAGNOSIS													
Sinusitis	1	.	2	.	.	.	.	.	.	.	1	.	4
Strep throat	3	2	1	2	6	1	1	2	.	.	1	2	21
Trichomoniasis	.	1	.	.	.	.	.	.	.	.	.	.	1
Unknown virus	4	2	.	2	2	4	.	.	2	6	2	6	30
Viral hepatitis	3	.	.	.	.	.	.	.	.	.	.	.	3

3

Infectious Diseases at Other sites

Year-to-date	MONTHLY TOTALS												TOTAL TO DATE
	JAN86	FEB86	MAR86	APR86	MAY86	JUN86	JUL86	AUG86	SEP86	OCT86	NOV86	DEC86	
DIAGNOSIS													
(Non-infectious)	3	4	3	5	2	13	7	9	7	3	4	1	61
Common cold	.	.	.	2	.	2	.	.	1	.	1	.	6
Genital candidiasis	.	.	.	.	.	.	.	.	.	.	.	1	1
Infectious colitus	.	.	.	.	1	.	.	.	.	.	.	1	2
Pulmonary TB	.	.	.	.	.	.	.	.	.	1	.	.	1
Strep throat	.	.	.	.	.	.	.	.	.	.	1	.	1

```
Infectious Diseases at Adolescent Center                                              4
------------------------------------------------------------------------------------
|Year-to-date    |                       MONTHLY TOTALS                   |TOTAL|
|                |-------------------------------------------------------| TO  |
|                | JAN86 | FEB86 | MAR86 | APR86 | MAY86 | JUN86 | AUG86 | SEP86 | OCT86 | NOV86 |DATE |
|----------------+-------+-------+-------+-------+-------+-------+-------+-------+-------+-------+-----|
|DIAGNOSIS       |       |       |       |       |       |       |       |       |       |       |     |
|----------------|       |       |       |       |       |       |       |       |       |       |     |
|(Non-infectious)|     1|     1|     5|     1|     1|     1|     3|     4|     6|     2|   25|
|----------------+-------+-------+-------+-------+-------+-------+-------+-------+-------+-------+-----|
|Common cold     |     .|     .|     .|     .|     .|     .|     .|     1|     .|     .|    1|
|----------------+-------+-------+-------+-------+-------+-------+-------+-------+-------+-------+-----|
|Pulmonary TB    |     .|     1|     2|     .|     .|     .|     1|     1|     .|     .|    5|
------------------------------------------------------------------------------------
```

EXAMPLE 5: STUDY OF ACTIVITY BY WEEKDAY

This example illustrates a technique for summarizing an entire year's worth of data into totals for each day of the week. The seven days of the week make a manageable number of classes for analyzing the total or average activity per weekday.

The code used to generate this table is shown below. For more information on the input data set and user-written formats used in this code, refer to **Formatting the Data**. The circled numbers to the left of the code indicate important coding techniques that are discussed in detail following the code. The output from this code is shown in **Output 6.7**.

```
    DATA TEMP;
       SET IN.CLINIC;
       KEEP DAY SITE;
❶     DAY=WEEKDAY(VISTDATE);
    PROC TABULATE DATA=TEMP FORMAT=6. MISSING;
       CLASS SITE DAY;
❷     FORMAT DAY DAYFORM. SITE  $SITE.;
       TABLE SITE='Location of clinic'  ALL='All clinics',
           DAY='Day of Visit'*
❸         (N='# of visits' PCTN<DAY>='% of week')
           / RTS=20;
    RUN;
```

1. This DATA step uses the WEEKDAY function to determine from each VISTDATE what day of the week the visit occurred. The new variable, DAY, permits you to summarize an entire year of data with seven classes representing the days of the week. This allows you to study activity by days of the week.
2. The FORMAT statement associates the numeric values stored in the new variable, DAY, with a user-defined format that gives descriptive names to the weekdays. Refer to **Formatting the Data** for a detailed description of the DAYFORM. format.
3. This denominator definition tells TABULATE that you want the percentage of the value in a single cell to the total for the row that contains the cell. Thus, you produce the percentage of one day's activity to the activity for the entire week. Note that this TABLE statement actually requests two statistics: the number of visits and the percentage of those visits to the entire week. Compare this TABLE statement to the one in the next example.

Output 6.7   Weekday Activity at the Clinic

	Day of Visit												
	Sunday		Monday		Tuesday		Wednesday		Thursday		Friday		Saturday	
	# of visits	% of week	# of visits	% of week	# of visits	% of week	# of visits	% of week	# of visits	% of week	# of visits	% of week	# of visits	% of week
Location of clinic														
Adolescent Center	2	7	2	7	.	.	3	10	6	21	10	34	6	21
Other sites	16	25	.	.	.	.	11	17	2	3	22	35	12	19
Main Clinic	231	16	192	14	11	1	242	17	242	17	237	17	251	18
All clinics	249	17	194	13	11	1	256	17	250	17	269	18	269	18

EXAMPLE 6: FOCUSING ON THE PRIMARY OUTPUT

As in example 2, this example simply illustrates how you can reformat a table to convey information differently. In this case, the table in **Output 6.7** contains so many numbers that it is difficult to distinguish totals from percentages. Because the percentages are the primary information in the table, **Output 6.8** prints only those values and omits the totals that were used to arrive at the percentages.

The code used to generate this table is shown below. For more information on the input data set, TEMP, refer to example 5 above. The formats, DAYFORM. and $SITE., are discussed in **Formatting the Data**. The circled number to the left of the code indicates an important coding technique that is discussed in detail following the code. The output from this code is shown in **Output 6.8**.

```
PROC TABULATE DATA=TEMP FORMAT=6. MISSING;
   CLASS SITE DAY;
   FORMAT DAY DAYFORM. SITE  $SITE.;
   TABLE SITE='Location of clinic'  ALL='All clinics',
      DAY='Percentage of Visits Each Weekday'*
❶    PCTN<DAY>=' '*F=9.
      / RTS=20;
RUN;
```

1. This TABLE statement differs from the one in the preceding example because the only statistic it requests is PCTN. It omits the N statistic. In this case the primary information to be conveyed is the relative percentage of activity. Printing both the actual number of visits and the percentage, as shown in **Output 6.7**, makes it difficult to read the table. The table in **Output 6.8** conveys the primary information more clearly.

Output 6.8 Percentage of Activity by Weekday

```
------------------------------------------------------------------------------------
|                   |              Percentage of Visits Each Weekday                |
|                   |-------------------------------------------------------------- |
|                   | Sunday  | Monday  | Tuesday |Wednesday|Thursday | Friday  |Saturday |
|-------------------+---------+---------+---------+---------+---------+---------+---------|
|Location of clinic |         |         |         |         |         |         |         |
|-------------------|         |         |         |         |         |         |         |
|Adolescent Center  |       7 |       7 |       . |      10 |      21 |      34 |      21 |
|-------------------+---------+---------+---------+---------+---------+---------+---------|
|Other sites        |      25 |       . |       . |      17 |       3 |      35 |      19 |
|-------------------+---------+---------+---------+---------+---------+---------+---------|
|Main Clinic        |      16 |      14 |       1 |      17 |      17 |      17 |      18 |
|-------------------+---------+---------+---------+---------+---------+---------+---------|
|All clinics        |      17 |      13 |       1 |      17 |      17 |      18 |      18 |
------------------------------------------------------------------------------------
```

Chapter 7

A Multiple-Response Example

This sample application uses a hypothetical survey to illustrate how multiple-response questions can be analyzed with PROC TABULATE. The DATA step processing required to prepare the data for TABULATE processing is discussed for each type of report produced.

Recommended Use

All users: refer to this chapter for illustrations of techniques described in the rest of the book. This chapter describes some special DATA step techniques for users who are using TABULATE to report the results of multiple-response surveys.

Contents

Figures

PURPOSE OF THE EXAMPLE

This example illustrates a number of coding techniques that are useful in handling the data generated by multiple-response surveys. In addition, this chapter illustrates many of the features of PROC TABULATE. In this sample application, you will find examples of

- methods for tracking the number of forms completed in the survey
- how to treat related variables that contain the possible responses to a question so that they form a unified group
- how to rearrange the basic data to permit crosstabulations of several multiple-response questions
- how to create the denominator definition to produce the percentage of one response to the total number surveyed
- techniques for altering the appearance of the table
- how to use the page dimension to produce descriptive headings for tables that would typically be two-dimensional
- methods of formatting the values of class variables to create classes.

THE SURVEY

An automobile manufacturer wants to analyze what influences people to buy their cars. Management wants to know which of several factors the buying public perceives to be important:

- cost
- performance
- reliability
- accessories
- exterior design.

In addition to information on their product, management wants to know how effective their advertising strategy has been and in particular what medium has most interested buyers in their product:

- newspaper advertisement
- magazine advertisement
- television advertisement
- talking to other people.

Assuming that magazines are a major forum for advertisements, management wants to know what magazines are the best places to advertise. And finally, they want to know the income level of the people who buy their product.

To obtain this information, the company decides to survey people in their showrooms. An analyst is assigned to create a survey form and produce the desired reports. The analyst begins by planning the reports needed by management:

- a summary report that lists each major factor and shows how many (by count and percentage) people selected each factor
- a listing of all other factors identified as important, providing the same information as Report 1
- a comparison of how people learned of the product and the major factors influencing their choice

- a comparison of the people who chose magazines as a major source of information to their preferences in magazines
- a detailed study of how the factors influencing the buyer's choice relate to the other data: income, source of information, and preferred magazines.

To produce these reports, the analyst designs the form illustrated in **Figure 7.1**.

ID#: XXXXXX

Please help us to serve you better by answering these questions.

What model car are you looking at today?

_____

What factors lead you to be interested in this car?

___Cost ___Performance ___Reliability

___Accessories ___Exterior design

Other:_____

Where did you find out about this car?

___Newspaper ___Magazine ___Television ___Word of mouth

Other:_____

What is your favorite magazine? (Select no more than two.)

___Newsweek ___Time ___Life ___Mother Jones

Other:_____

What is your annual household income?

___Under $10,000 ___$10,000-$25,000 ___$25,000-$40,000

___$40,000-$55,000 ___Over $55,000

Figure 7.1   Survey of Customers Purchasing Automobiles

PREPARING THE BASIC DATA

From this information, data entry personnel created a SAS data set containing the following variables:

ID a unique number identifying each survey form

FACTOR1 a numeric variable set to one or missing to indicate the presence or absence of factor 1, cost

FACTOR2 a numeric variable set to one or missing to indicate the presence or absence of factor 2, performance

FACTOR3 a numeric variable set to one or missing to indicate the presence or absence of factor 3, reliability

FACTOR4 a numeric variable set to one or missing to indicate the presence or absence of factor 4, accessories

FACTOR5 a numeric variable set to one or missing to indicate the presence or absence of factor 5, exterior design

F_OTHER the first 20 characters describing some other factor or blank

SOURCE1 a numeric variable set to one or missing to indicate the presence or absence of source 1, newspaper

SOURCE2 a numeric variable set to one or missing to indicate the presence or absence of source 2, magazine

SOURCE3 a numeric variable set to one or missing to indicate the presence or absence of source 3, television

SOURCE4 a numeric variable set to one or missing to indicate the presence or absence of source 4, word of mouth

S_OTHER the first 20 characters describing some other source or blank

MAGZIN1 1, 2, 3, or 4 for Newsweek, Time, Life or Mother Jones to indicate the first magazine choice

MAGZIN2 1, 2, 3, or 4 for Newsweek, Time, Life or Mother Jones to indicate the second magazine choice

M_OTHER the first 20 characters describing some other magazine or blank

INCOME a number between one and five indicating the level of income.

In addition to the data entered from the form, several other variables can be created to make processing easier. For example, if the respondent identified a factor other than the ones listed, it is useful to have a flag to indicate that Other was completed. So in the DATA step that creates the SAS data set, three more variables (FACTOR6, SOURCE5, and MAGZIN3) are created to indicate the presence or absence of Other information.

Refer to the sample data illustrated in **Figure 7.2** as you study this DATA step. **Output 7.1** shows the output from PROC CONTENTS after the SAS data set is created by the following code:

```
DATA IN.MULTRESP;
   INFILE RAW;
   LENGTH ID 8
          FACTOR1 FACTOR2 FACTOR3 FACTOR4
          FACTOR5 FACTOR6 2 F_OTHER $20
          SOURCE1 SOURCE2 SOURCE3 SOURCE4 SOURCE5 2 S_OTHER $20
          MAGZIN1 MAGZIN2 MAGZIN3 2 M_OTHER $20 INCOME 2;
   INPUT  ID FACTOR1 FACTOR2 FACTOR3 FACTOR4 FACTOR5 @16 F_OTHER $16.
          SOURCE1 SOURCE2 SOURCE3 SOURCE4 @41 S_OTHER $16.
          MAGZIN1 MAGZIN2 @62 M_OTHER $16. INCOME;
   IF F_OTHER¬=' ' THEN FACTOR6=1;
                   ELSE FACTOR6=.;
   IF S_OTHER¬=' ' THEN SOURCE5=1;
                   ELSE SOURCE5=.;
   IF M_OTHER¬=' ' THEN MAGZIN3=1;
                   ELSE MAGZIN3=.;
RUN;
```

Figure 7.2 illustrates the first thirty lines of raw data.

```
1001 1 . 1 . .  GOOD GAS MILEAGE 1 1 1 1 BILLBOARD        4 1             1
1002 1 . . . .  LOTS OF ROOM     1 1 1 1                   1 4             2
1003 . . . . .  FOUR WHEEL DRIVE 1 1 1 1                   4 1 PEOPLE      5
1004 1 1 1 1 1                   1 1 1 1                   3 1             5
1005 . . . . .  FOUR WHEEL DRIVE 1 1 1 1                   2 3             5
1006 1 1 1 1 1                   1 1 1 1                   2 1             1
1007 . . . . .  FOUR WHEEL DRIVE 1 1 1 1                   2 1 NEW REPUBLIC 3
1008 1 1 1 . 1                   1 1 1 1                   2 4             5
1009 1 1 1 . 1                   1 1 1 1                   2 1             1
1010 . . . . .  FOUR WHEEL DRIVE 1 1 1 1                   . .             1
1011 1 1 1 . 1                   1 1 1 1                   1 4 NEW YORKER   1
1012 1 1 1 1 1                   1 1 1 1                   2 1             1
1013 1 1 1 . .                   1 1 1 1                   1 4             3
1014 . . . . .  FOUR WHEEL DRIVE 1 1 1 1                   4 1             1
1015 1 1 1 . 1                   1 1 1 1                   1 3             1
1016 1 1 1 . 1                   1 1 1 1                   4 1             5
1017 1 . . . .  LOTS OF ROOM     1 1 1 1                   . .             5
1018 1 1 1 1 1                   1 1 1 1                   3 2             1
1019 1 . . . .  LOTS OF ROOM     1 1 1 1                   3 .             1
1020 1 1 1 . .                   1 1 1 1                   3 .             1
1021 1 1 1 1 1                   1 1 1 1                   . .             1
1022 1 1 1 . 1                   1 1 1 1                   1 4             3
1023 1 1 1 1 1                   1 1 1 1                   4 .             1
1024 1 1 1 . .                   1 1 1 1                   4 3             2
1025 1 1 1 . 1                   1 1 1 1                   3 2             5
1026 1 1 1 . 1                   1 1 1 1                   4 2             1
1027 1 1 1 1 1                   1 1 1 1                   3 2             2
1028 1 1 1 . 1                   1 1 1 1                   . .             1
1029 1 1 1 1 1                   1 1 1 1                   3 1             1
1030 1 1 1 1 1                   1 1 1 1                   4 1             4
```

Figure 7.2   Sample Input from Raw Data File

The PROC CONTENTS listing below shows the variables created by the DATA step as well as the variables from the raw data file.

Output 7.1   PROC CONTENTS Listing of MULTRESP Data Set

```
                              SAS

                        CONTENTS PROCEDURE
                  CONTENTS OF SAS MEMBER IN.MULTRESP


CREATED BY OS JOB TABMULT   ON CPUID 12-3456-789000
AT 15:20 FRIDAY, FEBRUARY 6, 1987   BY SAS RELEASE 5.16
DSNAME=ABCDEF.MISC.SASDATA OBSERVATIONS PER TRACK =460 BLKSIZE=23464
LRECL=102   GENERATED BY DATA
NUMBER OF OBSERVATIONS: 939   NUMBER OF VARIABLES: 19
MEMTYPE:   DATA

              ----ALPHABETIC LIST OF VARIABLES AND ATTRIBUTES-----
        #  VARIABLE  TYPE  LENGTH POSITION FORMAT      INFORMAT   LABEL
        8  F_OTHER   CHAR    20      24
        2  FACTOR1   NUM      2      12
        3  FACTOR2   NUM      2      14
        4  FACTOR3   NUM      2      16
        5  FACTOR4   NUM      2      18
        6  FACTOR5   NUM      2      20
        7  FACTOR6   NUM      2      22
        1  ID        NUM      8       4
       19  INCOME    NUM      2     100
       18  M_OTHER   CHAR    20      80
       15  MAGZIN1   NUM      2      74
       16  MAGZIN2   NUM      2      76
       17  MAGZIN3   NUM      2      78
       14  S_OTHER   CHAR    20      54
        9  SOURCE1   NUM      2      44
       10  SOURCE2   NUM      2      46
       11  SOURCE3   NUM      2      48
       12  SOURCE4   NUM      2      50
       13  SOURCE5   NUM      2      52
```

WORKING WITH A MULTIPLE-RESPONSE QUESTION

A major problem in dealing with multiple-response questions is how to handle a varying number of responses to a single question. Specific problems that arise are

- how do you compare the number of times each response is selected to the total number of surveys completed?
- how can you represent the separate variables that contain all possible responses as a unified group of responses to a single question?
- how do you report the varying responses to fill-in-the-blank questions, such as Other?

This section discusses methods of handling these separate variables and techniques for totalling all summary forms.

Example 1: Comparing Each Response to the Total Respondents

After gathering the data, the analyst prepares the reports requested by management. The primary question in the survey is the influence certain factors have on a buyer's choice. Because more than one factor can be influential, the analyst must be able to consider all selected factors. The separate variables for each possible response to a question allow each survey form to have as many selections as there are choices available. The first report is simply a tally of how many times each factor was selected and a comparison of that factor to the total number of forms completed. A sketch of the desired report might look like **Figure 7.3**.

```
                              Totals
                              ------
     Factors
     -------
        cost                  number who selected this factor
                              % of these to total respondents

        performance                    .
                                       .

        reliability                    .
                                       .

        accessories                    .
                                       .

        exterior design                .
                                       .

        other                          .
                                       .
```

Figure 7.3   Sketch of Report Showing Factors Affecting Choice

Although this report is relatively simple, it requires a piece of information that can be somewhat difficult to obtain without an extra DATA step: the total number of survey forms completed. The trick to obtaining this count is to

- identify a numeric variable that occurs in every observation (Note that it does not have to have unique values.)
- define this variable as an analysis variable by specifying it in the VAR statement
- use the variable as the denominator definition for the PCTN statistic.

Be sure to define the variable as an analysis variable. If you define it as a class variable, TABULATE treats each unique value of the variable as a separate class and provides totals by class instead of an overall total.

This technique of using an identifying number to tally the respondents is used in the following code. This code is the TABULATE solution to creating the output sketched in **Figure 7.3**. The circled numbers to the left of the code indicate other important coding techniques that are discussed in detail after the code. The output from this code is shown in **Output 7.2**.

```
❶ PROC TABULATE DATA=IN.MULTRESP FORMAT=9.2;
❷     VAR ID FACTOR1 FACTOR2 FACTOR3 FACTOR4 FACTOR5 FACTOR6;
❸     TABLE ALL='TOTAL NUMBER OF RESPONSE FORMS'*N=' '*F=5.
❹          (FACTOR1 FACTOR2 FACTOR3 FACTOR4 FACTOR5 FACTOR6)*
❺          (N*F=5. PCTN<ID>= '% OF RESPONDENTS'),
           ALL='TOTAL RESPONSES'
❻          / RTS=38 BOX='STUDY OF FACTORS AFFECTING CHOICE';
❼     KEYLABEL N='COUNT';
```

```
LABEL FACTOR1='COST'
      FACTOR2='PERFORMANCE'
      FACTOR3='RELIABILITY'
      FACTOR4='ACCESSORIES'
      FACTOR5='EXTERIOR DESIGN'
      FACTOR6='OTHER';
RUN;
```

1. The FORMAT=9.2 option establishes the default format for the table. The format modifier F=5., which appears twice in the TABLE statement, overrides the 9.2 format for all of the N statistics. The PCTN statistics default to the 9.2 format.
2. The ID variable and each of the factor variables are named in the VAR statement, which identifies them as analysis variables. Although the report requests only N and PCTN statistics, using these variables as analysis variables tells TABULATE not to create a category for each value that occurs. Note that all of these variables must be numeric.
3. The ALL variable used in the row dimension summarizes all of the observations and provides the total frequency of the observations. This same information can be obtained by replacing ALL with ID*N at this location in the table.
4. FACTOR1 through FACTOR6 are concatenated in the row dimension so that they appear to be six values of a single question: factors affecting choice. Because they are treated as analysis variables, the report only tallies the number of nonmissing values for them. If they were identified as class variables, each factor would have two values reported: the number selected and the number missing.
5. This report requests two statistics: the frequency that a single factor was selected and the percentage of that frequency to the total number of responses. The percentage requested for this table is simply the comparison of each factor to the total number of respondents. To obtain the total respondents, simply summarize how often ID occurs.
6. The BOX= option is used in this case to insert a literal value in the top left corner of the table.
7. The KEYLABEL statement defines a label to be used instead of N when N occurs in the output. The value defined in this statement is overridden by label assignments in the TABLE statement. Thus, N is replaced with a blank when it is crossed with ALL in the row dimension, but it is replaced with COUNT for all other occurrences.

Output 7.2   Report of Factors Affecting Choice

```
--------------------------------------------------
|STUDY OF FACTORS AFFECTING CHOICE   |  TOTAL   |
|                                    |RESPONSES |
|-----------------+------------------+----------|
|TOTAL NUMBER OF  |                  |          |
|RESPONSE FORMS   |                  |      939 |
|-----------------+------------------+----------|
|COST             |COUNT             |      756 |
|                 |------------------+----------|
|                 |% OF RESPONDENTS  |    80.51 |
|-----------------+------------------+----------|
|PERFORMANCE      |COUNT             |      560 |
|                 |------------------+----------|
|                 |% OF RESPONDENTS  |    59.64 |
|-----------------+------------------+----------|
|RELIABILITY      |COUNT             |      665 |
|                 |------------------+----------|
|                 |% OF RESPONDENTS  |    70.82 |
|-----------------+------------------+----------|
|ACCESSORIES      |COUNT             |      283 |
|                 |------------------+----------|
|                 |% OF RESPONDENTS  |    30.14 |
|-----------------+------------------+----------|
|EXTERIOR DESIGN  |COUNT             |      473 |
|                 |------------------+----------|
|                 |% OF RESPONDENTS  |    50.37 |
|-----------------+------------------+----------|
|OTHER            |COUNT             |      379 |
|                 |------------------+----------|
|                 |% OF RESPONDENTS  |    40.36 |
--------------------------------------------------
```

Example 2: Examining "Other" Responses

The second report requested by management is a list of all other factors listed on the survey forms. This report has the format illustrated in **Figure 7.4**.

```
                                       Totals
                                       ------

Other Factors
-------------
   ...                      number who selected this factor
                           % of these to total respondents

   ...                      number who selected this factor
                           % of these to total respondents
```

Figure 7.4   Sketch of Report Showing Other Factors Affecting Choice

This report focuses on the different values for a single variable: F_OTHER. Thus, it is appropriate to treat F_OTHER as a class variable to examine all the unique values for this variable.

The following code prints the table shown in **Output 7.3**. The circled numbers to the left of the code indicate important coding techniques that are discussed in detail following the code.

```
❶ PROC TABULATE DATA=IN.MULTRESP FORMAT=9.2;
     VAR ID;
❷   CLASS F_OTHER;
     TABLE ALL='TOTAL NUMBER OF OTHER RESPONSES'*N=' '*F=5.
         F_OTHER='OTHER FACTORS AFFECTING CHOICE'
❸       *(N*F=5.0 PCTN<F_OTHER*ID>='% OF RESPONDENTS'),
         ALL='TOTAL RESPONSES'
         / RTS=38;
     KEYLABEL N='COUNT';
  RUN;
```

1. The PROC TABULATE statement in this example does not include the
   MISSING option. Thus, only the surveys that provided a response for
   Other factors are reported. If you choose to specify the MISSING
   option, the percentages and totals in the table will be based on the total
   number of respondents. In addition, another category will be reported
   for missing values.
2. The F_OTHER variable is treated as a class variable so that a separate
   category is reported for each unique response.
3. The percentages produced by this denominator definition are relative to
   the number of survey forms that completed the Other space on the
   form. Refer to 1.

Output 7.3 Report of Other Factors Affecting Choice

```
-----------------------------------------------------
|                        |       | TOTAL   |
|                        |       |RESPONSES|
|------------------------|-------|---------|
|TOTAL NUMBER OF         |       |         |
|OTHER RESPONSES         |       |    379  |
|------------------------|-------|---------|
|OTHER FACTORS           |       |         |
|AFFECTING CHOICE        |       |         |
|------------------------|-------|---------|
|FOUR WHEEL DRIVE |COUNT         |    183  |
|                 |------------- |---------|
|                 |% OF RESPONDENTS|  48.28 |
|------------------------|---------------|---------|
|GOOD GAS MILEAGE |COUNT         |    105  |
|                 |------------- |---------|
|                 |% OF RESPONDENTS|  27.70 |
|------------------------|---------------|---------|
|LOTS OF ROOM     |COUNT         |     91  |
|                 |------------- |---------|
|                 |% OF RESPONDENTS|  24.01 |
-----------------------------------------------------
```

EXPANDING THE EXAMPLE

Analyzing and comparing results from several multiple-response questions
requires some reorganization of the data. This section shows how to do that.

Example 3: Combining Several Multiple–Response Questions

The next report to be produced from this survey is a comparison of how people
learned of the product and the major factors that influenced their choice. A sketch
of this report is illustrated in **Figure 7.5**.

```
                    Sources of Information
                    ---------------------

                ( list each source )   Other    None    Total
    Factors
    -------
      cost      number who selected    same     same    same
                   both of these       info     info    info
                % of this cell to      same     same    same
                   total respondents   info     info    info


    performance         .               .        .        .
                        .               .        .        .


    reliability         .               .        .        .
                        .               .        .        .


    accessories         .               .        .        .
                        .               .        .        .


    exterior            .               .        .        .
    design              .               .        .        .


    other               .               .        .        .
                        .               .        .        .
```

Figure 7.5 Sketch of Comparison of Factors Affecting Choice to Sources of Information

The variables FACTOR1 through FACTOR6 can again be treated as analysis variables and concatenated in the same dimension, but the variables for the remaining questions must be class variables. (Remember that all analysis variables must appear in the same dimension.) The five variables providing source of information responses need to be treated as a single variable with five possible responses. Because a single observation might have more than one source identified, the original data is reshaped as follows:

- A new class variable, RESPONSE, is created from the five related variables SOURCE1-SOURCE5.
- The values of the new variable are 1 through 4, 99 to indicate a response of Other, or 999 to indicate missing.
- A separate observation is created for each source identified on each survey form.
- If no sources were selected on a form, a single observation is created with a missing value for the RESPONSE variable.

Creating separate observations for each response to a question introduces a new problem: how do you keep track of how many survey forms were completed? Note the use of the QID variable introduced in the DATA step below to solve this problem. Because each observation in the original data set is split into multiple observations by this DATA step, the ID variable can no longer be counted to determine how many people responded to the survey. This DATA step creates the QID variable and sets it to a nonmissing value each time it reads an observation from the original data set. If any additional observations are created from that same input observation, QID is set to missing for them. Thus, QID can be used as ID was used in the previous examples.

```
DATA COMPARE;
   SET IN.MULTRESP;
   DROP F_OTHER SOURCE1 SOURCE2 SOURCE3 SOURCE4 S_OTHER
        MAGZIN1 MAGZIN2 M_OTHER INCOME;
   IF FACTOR1 OR FACTOR2 OR FACTOR3 OR
      FACTOR4 OR FACTOR5 OR FACTOR6 THEN NORESP=.;
   ELSE NORESP=1;
   QID=1;
   RESPONSE=.;
   IF SOURCE1 THEN DO;
      RESPONSE=1;
      OUTPUT;
      QID=.;
      END;
   IF SOURCE2 THEN DO;
      RESPONSE=2;
      OUTPUT;
      QID=.;
      END;
   IF SOURCE3 THEN DO;
      RESPONSE=3;
      OUTPUT;
      QID=.;
      END;
   IF SOURCE4 THEN DO;
      RESPONSE=4;
      OUTPUT;
      QID=.;
      END;
   IF SOURCE5 THEN DO;
      RESPONSE=99;
      OUTPUT;
      QID=.;
      END;
   IF RESPONSE=. THEN DO;
      RESPONSE=999;
      OUTPUT;
      QID=.;
      END;
RUN;
```

The following PROC TABULATE statements produce a table that analyzes the interplay of what interests car buyers and where car buyers find out about cars. The table produced by this code is shown in **Output 7.4**. The circled numbers to the left of the code indicate important coding techniques that are discussed in detail following the code.

```
        PROC FORMAT;
❶         VALUE RFMT   1='NEWS-PAPER'
                       2='MAGAZINE'
                       3='TELE-VISION'
                       4='WORD OF MOUTH'
                      99='OTHER'
                     999='NO RESPONSE';
❷       VALUE INVALNUM 0-HIGH=' ';
        PROC TABULATE DATA=COMPARE FORMAT=8.2;
          CLASS RESPONSE;
❸         VAR QID FACTOR1 FACTOR2 FACTOR3 FACTOR4 FACTOR5 FACTOR6 NORESP;
          FORMAT RESPONSE RFMT.;
❹         TABLE ALL='STUDY OF FACTORS AFFECTING CHOICE'*
                ALL='SOURCE OF PRODUCT INFORMATION',
❺               QID=' '*N='TOTAL NUMBER SURVEYED'*F=INVALNUM.
                (FACTOR1 FACTOR2 FACTOR3 FACTOR4 FACTOR5 FACTOR6 NORESP)*
❻               (N='COUNT'*F=5.0 PCTN<RESPONSE*QID QID>='% OF RESPONDENTS'),
❼               RESPONSE ALL='TOTAL RESPONSES'*F=9.
                / RTS=38 MISSTEXT=' ';
          LABEL FACTOR1='COST'
                FACTOR2='PERFORMANCE'
                FACTOR3='RELIABILITY'
                FACTOR4='ACCESSORIES'
                FACTOR5='EXTERIOR DESIGN'
                FACTOR6='OTHER'
                NORESP='NO RESPONSE';
        RUN;
```

1. Because the responses to the question on source of information have been combined into one variable, RESPONSE, with different numeric values, the values of RESPONSE need to be formatted to produce meaningful output. Note that some format values are hyphenated to tell TABULATE where to break the word when headings are printed. If the entire word fits on a line, TABULATE does **not** remove the hyphen.

2. This format has a special use for removing misleading data from the table. Refer to 5 below for a more detailed discussion.

3. Note that the QID variable, which is explained prior to the DATA step that created the COMPARE data set, is used like the ID variable in the previous examples to determine how many people responded to the survey.

4. The ALL variables in the page dimension simply allow you to specify a descriptive heading. If you want, you can insert this heading in the top left corner of the table by using the BOX=_PAGE_ option.

5. The QID variable in the row dimension summarizes the total number of respondents when it is crossed with the ALL variable in the column dimension. But QID is also unavoidably crossed with the RESPONSE variable in the column dimension, which produces some meaningless totals. These totals can be blanked out by specifying the INVALNUM. format defined in the PROC FORMAT step for the table cells that contain meaningless data. Refer also to 7 below.

6. The denominator definition for the TABLE statement is included in the row dimension and defines two possible denominators. Both of these denominator definitions are necessary because the column dimension concatenates two class variables: RESPONSE and ALL. The first

denominator, RESPONSE*QID, is used for all of the crossings of row dimension variables with the RESPONSE variable. The second denominator, QID, is used when the row dimension variables are crossed with ALL.

7. When the QID variable is crossed with ALL, it produces the total number of respondents. The value to be printed in this cell is formatted with a valid numeric format, 9. This format overrides the format in the row dimension, INVALNUM., which produces blanks in all other table cells in this row. Refer to 5 above for more information.

Output 7.4   Comparison of Factors Affecting Choice to Sources of Information

```
STUDY OF FACTORS AFFECTING CHOICE
AND SOURCE OF PRODUCT INFORMATION
-------------------------------------------------------------------------------------------------
|                 |                |                            RESPONSE                         |          |
|                 |                |-----------------------------------------------------------|          |
|                 |                | NEWS- |        | TELE- |WORD OF|      |   NO   | TOTAL    |
|                 |                | PAPER |MAGAZINE|VISION | MOUTH | OTHER |RESPONSE|RESPONSES |
|-----------------+----------------+-------+--------+-------+-------+------+--------+----------|
|                 |TOTAL NUMBER    |       |        |       |       |      |        |          |
|                 |SURVEYED        |       |        |       |       |      |        |      939 |
|-----------------+----------------+-------+--------+-------+-------+------+--------+----------|
|COST             |COUNT           |   404 |    322 |   480 |   244 |   14 |   270  |    1734  |
|                 |----------------+-------+--------+-------+-------+------+--------+----------|
|                 |% OF RESPONDENTS| 43.02 |  34.29 | 51.12 | 25.99 | 1.49 |  28.75 |     185  |
|-----------------+----------------+-------+--------+-------+-------+------+--------+----------|
|PERFORMANCE      |COUNT           |   301 |    250 |   355 |   192 |    7 |   201  |    1306  |
|                 |----------------+-------+--------+-------+-------+------+--------+----------|
|                 |% OF RESPONDENTS| 32.06 |  26.62 | 37.81 | 20.45 | 0.75 |  21.41 |     139  |
|-----------------+----------------+-------+--------+-------+-------+------+--------+----------|
|RELIABILITY      |COUNT           |   357 |    288 |   426 |   221 |   12 |   233  |    1537  |
|                 |----------------+-------+--------+-------+-------+------+--------+----------|
|                 |% OF RESPONDENTS| 38.02 |  30.67 | 45.37 | 23.54 | 1.28 |  24.81 |     164  |
|-----------------+----------------+-------+--------+-------+-------+------+--------+----------|
|ACCESSORIES      |COUNT           |   154 |    129 |   174 |   100 |    5 |   106  |     668  |
|                 |----------------+-------+--------+-------+-------+------+--------+----------|
|                 |% OF RESPONDENTS| 16.40 |  13.74 | 18.53 | 10.65 | 0.53 |  11.29 |      71  |
|-----------------+----------------+-------+--------+-------+-------+------+--------+----------|
|EXTERIOR DESIGN  |COUNT           |   249 |    209 |   294 |   162 |    7 |   175  |    1096  |
|                 |----------------+-------+--------+-------+-------+------+--------+----------|
|                 |% OF RESPONDENTS| 26.52 |  22.26 | 31.31 | 17.25 | 0.75 |  18.64 |     117  |
|-----------------+----------------+-------+--------+-------+-------+------+--------+----------|
|OTHER            |COUNT           |   198 |    149 |   244 |   107 |   12 |   131  |     841  |
|                 |----------------+-------+--------+-------+-------+------+--------+----------|
|                 |% OF RESPONDENTS| 21.09 |  15.87 | 25.99 | 11.40 | 1.28 |  13.95 |      90  |
|-----------------+----------------+-------+--------+-------+-------+------+--------+----------|
|NO RESPONSE      |COUNT           |     0 |      0 |     0 |     0 |    0 |     0  |       0  |
|                 |----------------+-------+--------+-------+-------+------+--------+----------|
|                 |% OF RESPONDENTS|       |        |       |       |      |        |          |
-------------------------------------------------------------------------------------------------
```

Example 4: Another Look at "Other"

This report compares the preference in magazine to the source of information and focuses on those who selected magazines as a source of information. As in example 2, this report examines the contents of the Other category from the survey form. But in this case, a limited number of surveys are selected (only those who indicated magazines as a source of information). Then the contents of the Other category are combined with the standard responses to the question on magazine preference to get the total picture of preferences for the magazine-reading customers. A sketch of this report is illustrated in **Figure 7.6**.

```
                    Preferred Magazines
                    -------------------


                (list each magazine)        Total
  Sources
  -------
     magazine     number who selected       same
                    both of these           info
                 % of this cell to          same
                    total respondents       info
```

Figure 7.6   Sketch of Report Showing Magazine Preferences

Because this report focuses on a single response to one of the multiresponse questions, the data set for this report includes only those people who have selected Magazine as a source of information. As for the previous report, the QID variable is created to count the number of survey forms, but in this case it counts only the selected survey forms. To examine all magazines identified on the survey forms, the three variables, MAGZIN1, MAGZIN2, and M_OTHER, are combined into a single variable MAGAZINE.

```
DATA MAGPREF;
   SET IN.MULTRESP;
   DROP MAGZIN1 MAGZIN2 M_OTHER;
   LENGTH MAGAZINE $ 20;
   IF SOURCE2 THEN DO;
      QID=1;
      IF MAGZIN1=1 OR MAGZIN2=1 THEN DO;
         MAGAZINE='NEWSWEEK';
         OUTPUT;
         QID=.;
         END;
      IF MAGZIN1=2 OR MAGZIN2=2 THEN DO;
         MAGAZINE='TIME';
         OUTPUT;
         QID=.;
         END;
      IF MAGZIN1=3 OR MAGZIN2=3 THEN DO;
         MAGAZINE='LIFE';
         OUTPUT;
         QID=.;
         END;
      IF MAGZIN1=4 OR MAGZIN2=4 THEN DO;
         MAGAZINE='MOTHER JONES';
         OUTPUT;
         QID=.;
         END;
```

```
        IF MAGZIN3 THEN DO;
           MAGAZINE=M_OTHER;
           OUTPUT;
           QID=.;
           END;
        END;
  RUN;
```

The following PROC TABULATE statements produce a table that shows what percentage of the magazine-reading buyers read each type of magazine. The table produced by this code is shown in **Output 7.5**. The circled numbers to the left of the code indicate important coding techniques that are discussed in detail following the code.

```
     PROC TABULATE FORMAT=8.2 DATA=MAGPREF;
❶      CLASS MAGAZINE;
❷      VAR QID;
       TABLE (N='COUNT'*F=5.0
❸             PCTN<MAGAZINE*QID QID>='% OF RESPONDENTS'),
              MAGAZINE='FAVORITE MAGAZINE' QID='TOTAL READERS'
              / RTS=20;
❹      TITLE1 'PREFERENCES OF THOSE WHO SELECTED';
       TITLE2 'MAGAZINES AS A SOURCE OF INFORMATION';
     RUN;
```

1. The newly created variable, MAGAZINE, contains the name of the magazines selected from the form or entered in the space on the form for Other magazines. Because there are a limited number of values for this variable and you want to examine each value as a separate category of information, specify this variable in the CLASS statement.
2. The QID variable is used in much the same way as the previous example, but for this table it reports only the surveys that selected magazines as a source of information.
3. This TABLE statement uses some of the same techniques illustrated in previous examples. Two denominator definitions are specified because the column dimension concatentates two variables. The QID variable is used in both denominators to get the percentage of each magazine to the total number of forms. Note that the QID variable is included in the column dimension to obtain the count of all selected survey forms.
4. This PROC TABULATE step uses TITLE statements instead of specifying the title of the table in the page dimension, as illustrated in previous reports.

Output 7.5   Report of Magazine Preferences

```
PREFERENCES OF THOSE WHO SELECTED
MAGAZINES AS A SOURCE OF INFORMATION
------------------------------------------------------------------------------------
|                  |                          FAVORITE MAGAZINE                    |        |
|                  |-------------------------------------------------------|UNLISTED| TOTAL |
|                  | MOTHER | NEW    | NEW    |         |        |      | CHOICE |READERS |
|            | LIFE | JONES |REPUBLIC| YORKER |NEWSWEEK| PEOPLE | TIME |        |        |
|------------------+------+------+------+------+------+------+------+------+------|
|COUNT             |  147 |  129 |   13 |   13 |  137 |   13 |  116 |   76 |  399 |
|------------------+------+------+------+------+------+------+------+------+------|
|% OF RESPONDENTS  |36.84 |32.33 | 3.26 | 3.26 |34.34 | 3.26 |29.07 |19.05 |100.00|
------------------------------------------------------------------------------------
```

ADVANCED TECHNIQUES

Example 5: Combining Different Types of Questions

The final report produced from this survey examines responses from several different questions in a unified report format. A sketch of this report is illustrated in **Figure 7.7**.

```
                        Income level
                        ------------

                 (list each income level)        Total

Factors
-------
   cost          number who selected             same
                   both of these                 info
                 % of this cell to               same
                   total respondents             info


   (list
    all
  factors)
```

(Figure continued on next page)

```
                  Source of information
                  ---------------------

              (list each source)    None   Other   Total
Factors
-------
   cost      number who selected    same   same    same
               both of these        info   info    info
             % of this cell to      same   same    same
               total respondents    info   info    info

   (list
    all
  factors)
```

```
                   Favorite Magazines
                   ------------------

              (list each magazine)   None   Other   Total
Factors
-------
   cost      number who selected    same   same    same
               both of these        info   info    info
             % of this cell to      same   same    same
               total respondents    info   info    info

   (list
    all
  factors)
```

Figure 7.7   Sketch of Report Analyzing Answers to Several Multiple-
Response Questions

Keep in mind that the questions on the survey have varying types of responses.

- The questions on factors influencing the buyer's choice and sources of information are multiple-response questions that permit unlimited choices.
- The preferred magazine question permits a limited number of responses.
- The income question has only one response.

The difficulty with this report is producing a single table that includes all questions in a format that is meaningful for each question. Once again, before producing the table, you must reformat the data to make it more manageable. The DATA step below manipulates the input data set with the following techniques:

- The separate variables that store responses to questions (INCOME, SOURCE1 through SOURCE5, and MAGZIN1 through MAGZIN3) are recombined into two variables: QUESTION and RESPONSE. Together the codes in these variables indicate the question and a single response to it.

- Multiple observations are created for multiple responses.
- The QID variable is used, as in previous examples, to keep track of the actual number of surveys completed.

```
DATA SEVERAL;
   SET IN.MULTRESP;
   DROP F_OTHER SOURCE1 SOURCE2 SOURCE3 SOURCE4 SOURCE5 S_OTHER
        MAGZIN1 MAGZIN2 MAGZIN3 M_OTHER INCOME;
   IF FACTOR1 OR FACTOR2 OR FACTOR3 OR
      FACTOR4 OR FACTOR5 OR FACTOR6 THEN NORESP=.;
   ELSE NORESP=1;
   QUESTION=1;
   QID=1;
   IF      INCOME=1 THEN RESPONSE=1;
   ELSE IF INCOME=2 THEN RESPONSE=2;
   ELSE IF INCOME=3 THEN RESPONSE=3;
   ELSE IF INCOME=4 THEN RESPONSE=4;
   ELSE IF INCOME=5 THEN RESPONSE=5;
   ELSE IF INCOME=. THEN RESPONSE=999;
   ELSE                  RESPONSE=99;
   OUTPUT;
   QID=.;
   QUESTION=2;
   RESPONSE=.;
   IF SOURCE1 THEN DO;
      RESPONSE=6;
      OUTPUT;
      END;
   IF SOURCE2 THEN DO;
      RESPONSE=7;
      OUTPUT;
      END;
   IF SOURCE3 THEN DO;
      RESPONSE=8;
      OUTPUT;
      END;
   IF SOURCE4 THEN DO;
      RESPONSE=9;
      OUTPUT;
      END;
   IF SOURCE5 THEN DO;
      RESPONSE=99;
      OUTPUT;
      END;
   IF RESPONSE=. THEN DO;
      RESPONSE=999;
      OUTPUT;
      END;
   QUESTION=3;
   RESPONSE=.;
   IF      MAGZIN1=1 THEN RESPONSE=10;
   ELSE IF MAGZIN1=2 THEN RESPONSE=11;
   ELSE IF MAGZIN1=3 THEN RESPONSE=12;
   ELSE IF MAGZIN1=4 THEN RESPONSE=13;
   IF RESPONSE¬=. THEN OUTPUT;
```

```
       RESPONSE=.;
       IF      MAGZIN2=1 THEN RESPONSE=10;
       ELSE IF MAGZIN2=2 THEN RESPONSE=11;
       ELSE IF MAGZIN2=3 THEN RESPONSE=12;
       ELSE IF MAGZIN2=4 THEN RESPONSE=13;
       IF RESPONSE¬=. THEN OUTPUT;
       ELSE IF MAGZIN3 THEN DO;
          RESPONSE=99;
          OUTPUT;
          END;
       ELSE DO;
          RESPONSE=999;
          OUTPUT;
          END;
    RUN;
```

The PROC TABULATE statements below read the data set created by this DATA step and produce a table that analyzes three of the questions included on the survey form. The table produced by this code is shown in **Output 7.6**. The circled numbers to the left of the code indicate important coding techniques that are discussed in detail following the code.

```
       PROC FORMAT;
❶      VALUE QFMT 1='HOUSEHOLD INCOME'
                  2='SOURCE OF INFORMATION'
                  3='FAVORITE MAGAZINES';

❷      VALUE RFMT 1='UNDER 10,000'
                  2='10,000-25,000'
                  3='25,000-40,000'
                  4='40,000-55,000'
                  5='OVER 55,000'

                  6='NEWS-PAPER'
                  7='MAGAZINE'
                  8='TELE-VISION'
                  9='WORD OF MOUTH'

                 10='NEWSWEEK'
                 11='TIME'
                 12='LIFE'
                 13='MOTHER JONES'

                 99='OTHER'
                999='NO RESPONSE';

       VALUE INVALNUM 0-HIGH=' ';
     PROC TABULATE DATA=SEVERAL FORMAT=8.2;
❸      CLASS QUESTION RESPONSE;
❹      VAR QID FACTOR1 FACTOR2 FACTOR3 FACTOR4
           FACTOR5 FACTOR6 NORESP;
❺      FORMAT RESPONSE RFMT. QUESTION QFMT.;
```

❻   TABLE ALL='STUDY OF FACTORS AFFECTING CHOICE VERSUS'*QUESTION=' '
            QID=' '*SUM='TOTAL RESPONDENTS'*F=INVALNUM.
            (FACTOR1 FACTOR2 FACTOR3 FACTOR4 FACTOR5 FACTOR6 NORESP)*
            (N='COUNT'*F=5.0
❼   PCTN<QUESTION*RESPONSE*QID QUESTION*QID>
            ='% OF RESPONDENTS'),
            RESPONSE ALL='TOTAL RESPONSES'*F=9.
            / RTS=38 BOX='SEE FIRST LINE OF FIRST PAGE FOR TOTAL RESPONDENTS';
      LABEL FACTOR1='COST'
            FACTOR2='PERFORMANCE'
            FACTOR3='RELIABILITY'
            FACTOR4='ACCESSORIES'
            FACTOR5='EXTERIOR DESIGN'
            FACTOR6='OTHER'
            NORESP='NO RESPONSE';
   RUN;

1. This VALUE statement defines a format for the QUESTION variable created in the DATA step. These values represent the three classes of questions in the survey.
2. This VALUE statement defines a format for the RESPONSE variable created in the DATA step. This variable is more complex because it contains the values of all responses to all three classes of questions.
3. The CLASS statement defines both of the new variables as class variables. The classes of these variables form the page and column headings.
4. As in previous examples, the FACTOR variables and the QID variable are defined as analysis variables.
5. Be sure to include the FORMAT statement to make use of the formats defined in the PROC FORMAT step. Remember that formats defined in the FORMAT statement affect only the headings of the table, not the values in the table cells.
6. In this table, the page dimension has a real value (ALL*QUESTION) instead of just ALL associated with a descriptive heading. The complexity of this report requires that we use a three-dimensional table. The QUESTION variable breaks the report into separate pages for each question in the survey.
7. As the number of dimensions in the table increases, the denominator definition becomes more complex. For this table, you must cross QUESTION as well as RESPONSE with QID to get the total number of surveys. If the QUESTION variable is omitted, the denominator does not produce percentages based on the entire survey.

Output 7.6   Analysis of Answers to Several Multiple-Response Questions

```
STUDY OF FACTORS AFFECTING CHOICE VERSUS                                                    1
HOUSEHOLD INCOME
```

SEE FIRST LINE OF FIRST PAGE FOR TOTAL RESPONDENTS		RESPONSE					
		UNDER 10,000	10,000-25,000	25,000-40,000	40,000-55,000	OVER 55,000	TOTAL RESPONSES
	TOTAL RESPONDENTS						939
COST	COUNT	446	103	54	19	134	756
	% OF RESPONDENTS	47.50	10.97	5.75	2.02	14.27	81
PERFORMANCE	COUNT	327	73	37	13	110	560
	% OF RESPONDENTS	34.82	7.77	3.94	1.38	11.71	60
RELIABILITY	COUNT	390	88	46	18	123	665
	% OF RESPONDENTS	41.53	9.37	4.90	1.92	13.10	71
ACCESSORIES	COUNT	170	37	20	6	50	283
	% OF RESPONDENTS	18.10	3.94	2.13	0.64	5.32	30
EXTERIOR DESIGN	COUNT	279	61	30	13	90	473
	% OF RESPONDENTS	29.71	6.50	3.19	1.38	9.58	50
OTHER	COUNT	219	56	32	10	62	379
	% OF RESPONDENTS	23.32	5.96	3.41	1.06	6.60	40
NO RESPONSE	COUNT	0	0	0	0	0	0
	% OF RESPONDENTS	.	.	.	.	.	.

```
STUDY OF FACTORS AFFECTING CHOICE VERSUS                                                    2
SOURCE OF INFORMATION
```

SEE FIRST LINE OF FIRST PAGE FOR TOTAL RESPONDENTS		RESPONSE						
		NEWS-PAPER	MAGAZINE	TELE-VISION	WORD OF MOUTH	OTHER	NO RESPONSE	TOTAL RESPONSES
	TOTAL RESPONDENTS	.	.	.	.	.	.	.
COST	COUNT	404	322	480	244	14	270	1734
	% OF RESPONDENTS	43.02	34.29	51.12	25.99	1.49	28.75	185
PERFORMANCE	COUNT	301	250	355	192	7	201	1306
	% OF RESPONDENTS	32.06	26.62	37.81	20.45	0.75	21.41	139
RELIABILITY	COUNT	357	288	426	221	12	233	1537
	% OF RESPONDENTS	38.02	30.67	45.37	23.54	1.28	24.81	164
ACCESSORIES	COUNT	154	129	174	100	5	106	668
	% OF RESPONDENTS	16.40	13.74	18.53	10.65	0.53	11.29	71
EXTERIOR DESIGN	COUNT	249	209	294	162	7	175	1096
	% OF RESPONDENTS	26.52	22.26	31.31	17.25	0.75	18.64	117
OTHER	COUNT	198	149	244	107	12	131	841
	% OF RESPONDENTS	21.09	15.87	25.99	11.40	1.28	13.95	90
NO RESPONSE	COUNT	0	0	0	0	0	0	0
	% OF RESPONDENTS	.	.	.	.	.	.	.

```
STUDY OF FACTORS AFFECTING CHOICE VERSUS
FAVORITE MAGAZINES
```

SEE FIRST LINE OF FIRST PAGE FOR TOTAL RESPONDENTS		RESPONSE					TOTAL RESPONSES
		NEWSWEEK	TIME	LIFE	MOTHER JONES	OTHER	
	TOTAL RESPONDENTS	.	.	.	.	.	.
COST	COUNT	128	151	330	307	435	1351
	% OF RESPONDENTS	13.63	16.08	35.14	32.69	46.33	144
PERFORMANCE	COUNT	101	102	245	226	323	997
	% OF RESPONDENTS	10.76	10.86	26.09	24.07	34.40	106
RELIABILITY	COUNT	117	132	287	273	383	1192
	% OF RESPONDENTS	12.46	14.06	30.56	29.07	40.79	127
ACCESSORIES	COUNT	48	49	119	113	173	502
	% OF RESPONDENTS	5.11	5.22	12.67	12.03	18.42	53
EXTERIOR DESIGN	COUNT	86	84	205	188	278	841
	% OF RESPONDENTS	9.16	8.95	21.83	20.02	29.61	90
OTHER	COUNT	68	96	165	139	226	694
	% OF RESPONDENTS	7.24	10.22	17.57	14.80	24.07	74
NO RESPONSE	COUNT	0	0	0	0	0	0
	% OF RESPONDENTS	.	.	.	.	.	.

APPENDICES

Glossary of Terms for TABULATE
Processing

Answers to Common Questions

Glossary of Terms for TABULATE Processing

This appendix is a glossary that defines important terms used throughout this book. Keep in mind that the terms defined in this glossary may have other meanings outside of the context of TABULATE processing. This glossary defines these terms only as they relate to PROC TABULATE.

Recommended Use

All users: refer to this appendix for definitions of terms used in this guide.

ALL
> a universal class variable that represents a special summary class. All of the categories for class variables in the same parenthetical group or dimension (if ALL is not contained within a parenthetical group) are summarized by this variable.

analysis variable
> a variable identified in the VAR statement of the TABULATE procedure. An analysis variable must be numeric. It often contains quantitative or continuous values, but this is not a requirement. You can request a variety of descriptive statistics for analysis variables.

category
> the combination of unique values of class variables. TABULATE creates a separate category for each unique combination of values that exists in the observations of the data set. Each category created by TABULATE is represented by one or more cells in the table where the pages, rows, and columns that describe the category intersect.

cell
> a single unit of the table produced by TABULATE. The value contained in the cell is a summary statistic for the input data set. The contents of a cell are described by the page, row, and column that contain the cell.

class variable
> a variable identified in the CLASS statement of the TABULATE procedure. Class variables can have character, integer, or even continuous values, but they typically have a few discrete values that define the classifications of the variable.

column
> the vertical dimension of a table. The column dimension is the last dimension defined in the TABLE statement. If the TABLE statement contains only one dimension expression, the table has only column headings.

column concatenation
> two or more tables produced by one TABLE statement and juxtaposed side by side.

concatenation
> the operation that instructs TABULATE to join information for two or more elements by placing the output for the second element immediately after the output for the first element. Concatenated elements produce tables consisting of two or more subtables.

crossing
> the operation that instructs TABULATE to combine the effects of two or more elements. If the elements are class variables, TABULATE creates categories from the combination of values of the variables. If one of the elements is an analysis variable, the statistics for the analysis variable are calculated for the categories created by the class variables. Crossings are also used to apply formats to the values in the cells in a particular dimension.

denominator
> the part of a fraction below the dividing line.

denominator definition
: the expression or group of expressions that tells TABULATE what values should be used to calculate the denominator for the percentage you have requested. Omitting the denominator definition tells TABULATE to calculate the percentage of the value in one cell to the total for all categories in the table.

dimension
: the page, row, or column portion of a table. TABULATE can produce one-, two-, or three-dimensional tables.

dimension expression
: the portion of the TABLE statement that defines what variables and statistics make up a single dimension of the table. The format of a dimension expression is the same for any of the three dimensions: page, row, and column. Class variables can appear in all dimensions of the TABLE statement. Analysis variables can appear in any dimension, but all analysis variables must appear in the same dimension. The same is true for statistics: they can appear in any dimension, but all of them must be in the same dimension. Analysis variables and statistics do not have to be in the same dimension.

element
: a variable, a statistic, a format modifier, the universal class variable, ALL, or a combination produced by crossing two or more of these. Elements are used to create expressions in a TABLE statement.

format modifier
: an element of the form F=*format* that can be crossed in a dimension expression to indicate how the values in cells should be formatted.

heading
: a label that describes the contents of some portion of the table. TABULATE creates page, row, and column headings from the names and values of class variables, the names of analysis variables, keywords for statistics, and literal values.

label assignment
: a method of changing the default heading for a page, row, or column by assigning the new heading in the TABLE statement. A label assignment can change the name of a class or analysis variable or the name of a statistic. It cannot be used to change the values of a class variable. The format for a label assignment is

> *element*='*new label*'

where *element* is the name of the variable or statistic and *new label* is the label you want to assign for the heading.

logical page
: all of the rows and columns defined by a TABLE statement. A logical page can contain more rows and columns than can be printed on one physical page. If the logical page has to be broken into parts, each part prints on a separate physical page. When the logical pages are short, you can print several of them on one page by using the CONDENSE option.

missing value
: a special representation to indicate that a variable or a table cell has no value assigned to it. Missing values occur in SAS data sets when a variable has no value for an observation. Missing values appear in

tables produced by TABULATE when no observations have the combination of values that describe that table cell.

operators

symbols that indicate relationships between elements of a dimension expression. TABULATE provides operators for crossing, concatenating, and grouping elements, as well as an operator for assigning labels.

page

the dimension of a table that resembles the groupings produced by the BY statement. The page dimension is the first dimension defined in a three-dimensional TABLE statement.

PCTN

a statistic that provides the percentage of the frequency in a single cell to a total frequency. The total frequency used for computing the percentage is defined by the denominator definition that follows the PCTN statistic.

PCTSUM

a statistic that provides the percentage of the sum in a single cell to another total. The total used for computing the percentage is defined by the denominator definition that follows the PCTSUM statistic. This statistic can be requested only for analysis variables.

physical page

the portion of a table that is formatted to print on a single page of paper or a single screen. A physical page and a logical page may be the same, or a physical page may not contain the entire logical page, or it may contain several logical pages if the CONDENSE option is specified.

row

the horizontal dimension of a table. The row dimension is the next-to-the-last dimension of a table defined in the TABLE statement.

row concatenation

two or more tables produced by one TABLE statement and juxtaposed one above the other.

row title space (RTS)

the amount of space allotted for printing all of the headings for the row dimension of a table as well as two outlining characters. This space is divided equally among all levels of headings for the row dimension.

subtable

the group of cells produced by crossing a single element from each dimension of the TABLE statement when one or more dimensions contain concatenated elements. Each subtable of a larger table could be produced separately by rewriting the TABLE statement as several simple TABLE statements with no concatenated elements. This statement

    TABLE DEPT ALL,EXPENSE;

produces two subtables: DEPT*EXPENSE and ALL*EXPENSE.

table

the collection of cells that report the summary statistics for the categories described by the page, row, and column headings.

Answers to Common Questions

Many SAS users have similar difficulties using and understanding some of the capabilities of PROC TABULATE. This appendix describes some common mistakes that users make, explains what causes the errors, and offers solutions to the problems.

Recommended Use

All users: locate answers to questions that arise as you use PROC TABULATE.

Contents

Figures

Class or Analysis–Does It Make a Difference?

You might not be sure whether you want to define a variable as a class variable by including it in the CLASS statement, or as an analysis variable by naming it in the VAR statement. Keep in mind that all variables used in the TABLE statement must be specified in one of these two statements. Unlike the VAR statement in many SAS procedures, the VAR statement in PROC TABULATE is not used for all variables used by the procedure—only those that should be treated as analysis variables.

The question of how to treat variables has some far-reaching statistical implications. Refer to the **References** at the end of this appendix for detailed discussions of this topic. The checklists below can help you make some simple decisions about how to use a variable.

Define the variable in the CLASS statement if you want to

- print distinct values for the variable as page, row, or column headings
- group a cluster of values and then print a heading for this cluster. (Use PROC FORMAT to group values.)
- report how frequently each value of the variable occurs.

Define the variable in the VAR statement if you want to

- obtain descriptive statistics on the data
- obtain a single frequency count for all nonmissing values of the variable.

The following problems can occur when you define a variable as one type of variable and then use it like the other type of variable in the TABLE statement:

- Your table has an enormous number of columns or rows that you did not expect. This happens when you define a variable in the CLASS statement and it has too many unique values. You might actually want to use it as an analysis variable and request the N statistic. It is legitimate to declare a variable as an analysis variable when you only want to know how often the variable has nonmissing values. Or you might want to continue to use it as a class variable but also use PROC FORMAT to group some of the values into distinct classes.
- You get the message

`STATISTIC OTHER THAN N REQUESTED WITHOUT ANALYSIS VARIABLE.`

You need to define variables as analysis variables if you request the SUM, MEAN, or any statistic other than N or PCTN.
- You get the message

`MULTIPLE ANALYSIS VARIABLES IN A SINGLE NESTING.`

You must concatenate all analysis variables in the same dimension of the table, and you cannot cross two analysis variables. If you think you need to put the two variables in different dimensions, you probably need to make one of them a class variable.

Why Are Some Observations Omitted?

PROC TABULATE omits observations that have missing values for any of the variables defined in the CLASS statement. The CLASS statement affects all TABLE statements in a PROC TABULATE step. So, if you define a variable as a CLASS variable and then do not use it in a TABLE statement, TABULATE still omits observations that have missing values for that variable. Consider the following example:

```
DATA POLITIC;
    INPUT SEX $ RACE $ POLITICS $ GRADYEAR;
```

```
    CARDS;
 F B . 82
 F B D .
 M . D 70
 M W R .
 ;
 PROC TABULATE DATA=POLITIC;
    CLASS SEX RACE POLITICS GRADYEAR;
    TABLE RACE*SEX;
 RUN;
```

This code produces only the message

`WARNING: A CLASS, FREQ, OR WGT VARIABLE IS MISSING ON EVERY OBS.`

No output is produced because you have named all four variables in the CLASS statement. Even the observations that have values for both RACE and SEX are not included in the table because they are affected by all of the variables in the CLASS statement.

To correct this problem, remove the extra variables from the CLASS statement if they are not needed for any TABLE statements in the step. If you do need the variables in the CLASS statement, add the MISSING option to the PROC TABULATE statement so that all observations are included in the output.

Which Should I Use–MISSING, PRINTMISS, or MISSTEXT= ?

These three options are related, but they have distinctively different uses. As discussed above, use MISSING to ensure that all observations are included in the output for the table. MISSING tells TABULATE to include observations that have missing values for class variables.

Use PRINTMISS to ensure that page, row, and column headings are the same for all logical pages of the table. PRINTMISS tells TABULATE to print all values that occur for a class variable each time headings are printed for that variable. Note that PRINTMISS does not cause TABULATE to print rows or columns for values that are not present in the data set.

Use the MISSTEXT= option to define up to 20 characters of text that print in table cells when there are no observations that contain that combination of values for class variables. Note that MISSTEXT= does not relate to missing data values in the input data set; it operates only on the contents of the table cells.

The following examples illustrate each of these options and also show how these options interact. All of these examples use the data created in the DATA step listed in **Why Are Some Observations Omitted?**

The first example uses none of the options. As discussed in the preceding section, the problem in this example is that the CLASS statement names variables that are not needed in the TABLE statement. Because these extra variables have missing values, no observations are selected for the table.

```
 PROC TABULATE DATA=POLITIC;
    CLASS SEX RACE POLITICS GRADYEAR;
    TABLE RACE*SEX;
 RUN;
```

The output from this example is simply this message in the SAS log:

`WARNING: A CLASS, FREQ, OR WGT VARIABLE IS MISSING ON EVERY OBS.`

This example uses the same variables in the CLASS statement but includes the MISSING option in the PROC TABULATE statement:

```
PROC TABULATE DATA=POLITIC MISSING ;
   CLASS SEX RACE POLITICS GRADYEAR ;
   TABLE RACE*SEX;
RUN;
```

Thus, all observations are included in **Figure A2.1**.

```
-------------------------------------------
|                   RACE                   |
|------------------------------------------|
|         |       B       |      W         |
|---------+---------------+----------------|
|  SEX    |      SEX       |     SEX        |
|---------+---------------+----------------|
|   M     |      F        |      M         |
|---------+---------------+----------------|
|   N     |      N        |      N         |
|---------+---------------+----------------|
|    1.00 |         2.00  |        1.00     |
-------------------------------------------
```

Figure A2.1   Effect of MISSING Option

The next example eliminates the extra variable from the CLASS statement but does not include the MISSING option in the PROC TABULATE statement:

```
PROC TABULATE DATA=POLITIC;
   CLASS SEX RACE ;
   TABLE RACE*SEX;
RUN;
```

Thus, only the observations that have values for SEX and RACE are included in **Figure A2.2**.

```
---------------------------------
|             RACE              |
|------------------------------|
|      B      |       W        |
|-------------+----------------|
|     SEX     |      SEX       |
|-------------+----------------|
|      F      |       M        |
|-------------+----------------|
|      N      |       N        |
|-------------+----------------|
|       2.00  |         1.00   |
---------------------------------
```

Figure A2.2   Removing Extra Variables from the CLASS Statement

The example below eliminates the extra variable from the CLASS statement and requests that each class of a variable have the same headings. This example still includes only the observations that have values for SEX and RACE.

```
PROC TABULATE DATA=POLITIC;
   CLASS SEX RACE ;
   TABLE RACE*SEX / PRINTMISS ;
RUN;
```

The output from this code is illustrated in **Figure A2.3**.

```
--------------------------------------------------------------
|                            RACE                            |
|------------------------------------------------------------|
|              B               |              W              |
|------------------------------+-----------------------------|
|             SEX              |             SEX             |
|------------------------------+-----------------------------|
|      F       |       M       |       F       |      M      |
|--------------+---------------+---------------+-------------|
|      N       |       N       |       N       |      N      |
|--------------+---------------+---------------+-------------|
|         2.00 |            .  |            .  |        1.00 |
--------------------------------------------------------------
```

Figure A2.3   Effect of PRINTMISS Option

The next example uses both the MISSING option and the PRINTMISS option. Now all observations are included in the output, and the same headings appear for each class.

```
PROC TABULATE DATA=POLITIC MISSING FORMAT=9.;
   CLASS SEX RACE;
   TABLE RACE*SEX / PRINTMISS;
RUN;
```

The output from this code is illustrated in **Figure A2.4**.

```
----------------------------------------------------------------------------
|                                   RACE                                   |
|--------------------------------------------------------------------------|
|                  |              B              |            W             |
|------------------+-----------------------------+--------------------------|
|       SEX        |             SEX             |           SEX            |
|------------------+-----------------------------+--------------------------|
|   F    |    M    |    F    |    M    |    F    |    M    |
|--------+---------+---------+---------+---------+---------|
|   N    |    N    |    N    |    N    |    N    |    N    |
|--------+---------+---------+---------+---------+---------|
|     .  |      1  |      2  |      .  |      .  |      1  |
----------------------------------------------------------------------------
```

Figure A2.4   Using the MISSING and PRINTMISS Options

The following example uses the MISSING option, the PRINTMISS option, and the MISSTEXT= option. The output from this code, **Figure A2.5**, differs from **Figure A2.4** only in the text that appears for missing values in the table cells. Note that you must include both the PRINTMISS and the MISSTEXT= options to produce this output. If you omit PRINTMISS, there are no columns with missing values for the table cells, so the value for MISSTEXT= never appears.

```
PROC TABULATE DATA=POLITIC MISSING;
   CLASS SEX RACE AGE WEIGHT;
   TABLE RACE*SEX / PRINTMISS MISSTEXT='NONE';
RUN;
```

Figure A2.5 illustrates the output from this code.

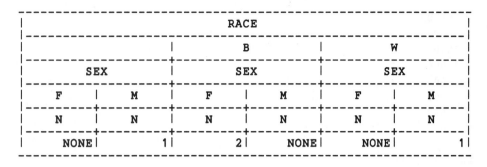

Figure A2.5   Using MISSING, PRINTMISS, and MISSTEXT= Options

How Do I Format This Table?

PROC TABULATE provides so many ways to format your table that knowing the best method is often difficult. If your table does not appear as you expected it to, check that you have followed these general guidelines:

- Use the FORMAT= option of the PROC TABULATE statement and the F= format modifiers in the TABLE statement to format the contents of table cells. Remember that the contents of the table cells represent summary statistics, not actual data values. You can format values in table cells with either SAS formats or user-written formats.
- Use the FORMAT statement to format the values of the class variables that make up page, row, and column headings. You can format headings with either SAS formats or user-written formats.
- Specifying an analysis variable in the FORMAT statement has no effect in PROC TABULATE. If you do this as an attempt to format the contents of the table cells, you need to use the methods described in the first item above instead.
- The width of a column is controlled by the FORMAT= option or the F= format modifier.
- The RTS= option defines the total amount of space for the row headings. If there are several levels of headings for rows, this space is divided equally among the levels. Remember that the RTS= value also includes two spaces for the outlining characters that enclose the row headings. So when you specify RTS=14, TABULATE can print twelve characters of heading in that space.

Why Are Some Headings Omitted?

If you use the PRINTMISS option, you might be surprised to find that some headings that you thought should appear in the row or column dimension do not appear. For example, if you specify a date format, such as DDMMYY., to print the dates in a month, your output does not automatically list every date in the month. Gaps may occur in the output because TABULATE prints headings only for the values that occur in the data set. If your data set does not include an observation for each day of the month, the output from TABULATE does not include headings for those days.

This rule holds true even when you create classes with PROC FORMAT. **TABULATE prints headings only for the values that actually occur in the data set.** For example, consider this DATA step and PROC TABULATE code:

```
DATA INPUT;
   INPUT DAY SALES;
```

```
        CARDS;
1 12000
1 15000
2 16000
2 15000
4 14000
4 11000
5 15000
;
PROC FORMAT;
   VALUE DAYMAT  1='MONDAY'
                 2='TUESDAY'
                 3='WEDNESDAY'
                 4='THURSDAY'
                 5='FRIDAY';
PROC TABULATE DATA=INPUT;
   CLASS DAY;
   VAR SALES;
   TABLE DAY,SALES;
   FORMAT DAY DAYMAT. ;
RUN;
```

This code produces the table shown in **Figure A2.6**. As you can see, the table does not include row headings for Wednesday because no observations occurred in the data set with a value of 3 for DAY.

```
-----------------------------------------------
|                              |    SALES    |
|                              |-------------|
|                              |    SUM      |
|------------------------------+-------------|
|DAY                           |             |
|------------------------------|             |
|MONDAY                        |   27000.00  |
|------------------------------+-------------|
|TUESDAY                       |   31000.00  |
|------------------------------+-------------|
|THURSDAY                      |   25000.00  |
|------------------------------+-------------|
|FRIDAY                        |   15000.00  |
-----------------------------------------------
```

Figure A2.6   Headings Omitted When Values Do Not Occur in the Data Set

Because Wednesday never occurs in the data set, adding the PRINTMISS option will have no effect on the output. To work around this problem, you can add some dummy observations for the values you want to insert in the data set. For example, in the following code, two steps have been added to the code that produces **Figure A2.6**: the DATA DUMMY step creates dummy observations, and the DATA FINISH step adds the dummy observations to the original data set.

```
DATA INPUT;
   INPUT DAY SALES;
   CARDS;
1 12000
1 15000
2 16000
```

```
  2 15000
  4 14000
  4 11000
  5 15000
  ;
PROC FORMAT;
   VALUE DAYMAT 1='MONDAY'
                2='TUESDAY'
                3='WEDNESDAY'
                4='THURSDAY'
                5='FRIDAY';
DATA DUMMY;
   SALES=0;
   DO DAY=1 TO 5;
      OUTPUT;
      END;
DATA FINISH;
   SET INPUT DUMMY;
PROC TABULATE DATA=FINISH;
   CLASS DAY;
   VAR SALES;
   TABLE DAY,SALES;
   FORMAT DAY DAYMAT.;
RUN;
```

The altered code produces the table shown in **Figure A2.7**.

```
------------------------------------------------
|                                | SALES       |
|                                |-------------|
|                                | SUM         |
|--------------------------------+-------------|
|DAY                             |             |
|--------------------------------|             |
|MONDAY                          |   27000.00  |
|--------------------------------+-------------|
|TUESDAY                         |   31000.00  |
|--------------------------------+-------------|
|WEDNESDAY                       |       0.00  |
|--------------------------------+-------------|
|THURSDAY                        |   25000.00  |
|--------------------------------+-------------|
|FRIDAY                          |   15000.00  |
------------------------------------------------
```

Figure A2.7   Forcing TABULATE to Print Omitted Headings

Why Are the Headings in This Order?

Several problems might cause headings to appear in an unexpected order. Keep in mind that the ORDER= option in the PROC TABULATE statement controls how headings for class variables appear in the output. By default, TABULATE orders class variables in ascending order of the actual data values. When you use the FORMAT statement to create the classes for a class variable, you should consider whether you also need to change the order of the headings by specifying ORDER=FORMATTED.

Occasionally, you want to order the headings for one variable by the actual data values and also order the headings for another variable by the formatted values. One method for doing this is to sort the data as you want it to appear and then specify ORDER=DATA. Note that this technique is not foolproof, however.

For this to work, the first value of the first variable to be sorted must occur with all possible values of the second variable. Problems occur when this requirement is not met. For example, if you have the following sorted values for two variables

ANIMAL	FOOD
CATS	FISH
CATS	MEAT
CATS	MILK
DOGS	BONES
DOGS	FISH
DOGS	MEAT

the headings for the table when you specify ORDER=DATA in the PROC TABULATE statement, as shown in this TABULATE step,

```
PROC TABULATE ORDER=DATA FORMAT=9.;
   CLASS ANIMAL FOOD;
   TABLE ANIMAL*FOOD;
RUN;
```

look like those in **Figure A2.8**.

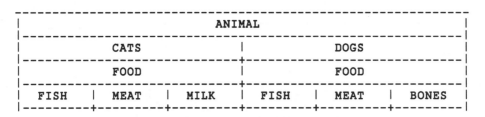

Figure A2.8   Ordering of Classes Remains Constant for Entire Data Set

For this table to appear in the correct order, the first value, CATS, would have to appear with all values of FOOD. Because BONES occurs only with DOG, TABULATE encounters this value after all FOOD values for CAT and prints it last.

Note that the order established by ORDER=DATA remains the same for the entire data set. If you need to have the ordering reestablished for different groups of data, use the BY statement.

What's Wrong with the Denominator?

If you have written TABLE statements that specify denominator definitions for PCTN and PCTSUM statistics, you have probably encountered the message:

`A PCTSUM CROSSING HAS NO DENOMINATOR IN TABLE OF LINE nn.`

To determine which crossing is causing the trouble, you need to list all the crossings generated by the TABLE statement and see which ones are omitted from the denominator definition.

Problems with denominator definitions occur most often when one or more of the table dimensions has several variables or crossings concatenated in the same dimension. For example, the following code is similar to an example from Chapter 6, but the code below produces the error message listed above:

```
PROC TABULATE;
   CLASS SITE PROV1;
   FORMAT SITE $SITE. PROV1 $PROVIDE.;
   VAR TOTBILL TOTDUE;
   TABLE SITE='Clinic location' ALL='All clinics',
        (PROV1=' ' ALL='Summary')*(N='# of visits'*F=5.
        TOTBILL='Worth of Services'*(MEAN SUM
        PCTSUM<SITE*PROV1
             SITE*ALL
             ALL*PROV1>
             ='% of worth to worth of all services')
        TOTDUE='Amount Billed'*
        (SUM PCTSUM<TOTBILL>='% of worth'*F=7.2))
        / RTS=12 CONDENSE;
   RUN;
```

To discover which of the crossings has no denominator, first simplify the TABLE statement by removing all of the format modifiers and label assignments. The simplified TABLE statement looks like this:

```
TABLE SITE ALL,
     (PROV1 ALL)*(N TOTBILL*(MEAN SUM
     PCTSUM<SITE*PROV1
          SITE*ALL
          ALL*PROV1>)
     TOTDUE*(SUM PCTSUM<TOTBILL>));
RUN;
```

Now you can list each crossing generated by the TABLE statement and determine if it has a denominator. First note that the following crossings are produced by the TABLE statement but **are not crossed with the PCTSUM statistic**, so they need no denominator definition.

```
SITE * PROV1 * N
SITE * ALL   * N
ALL  * PROV1 * N
ALL  * ALL   * N
```

In addition, these crossings have a separate denominator definition, which cannot be producing the problem because this denominator definition consists only of an analysis variable.

```
SITE * PROV1 * TOTDUE * PCTSUM<TOTBILL>
SITE * ALL   * TOTDUE * PCTSUM<TOTBILL>
ALL  * PROV1 * TOTDUE * PCTSUM<TOTBILL>
ALL  * ALL   * TOTDUE * PCTSUM<TOTBILL>
```

The crossings that are in question are listed below. Note that the PCTSUM element shows which portion of the complete denominator definition is used for each crossing.

```
SITE * PROV1 * PCTSUM<SITE*PROV1>
SITE * ALL   * PCTSUM<SITE*ALL>
ALL  * PROV1 * PCTSUM<ALL*PROV1>
ALL  * ALL   *         missing
```

As you can see from this list of crossings, the last set of crossings have no denominator. You need to add ALL to the denominator definition to correct the TABLE statement. Thus, the corrected denominator definition is

```
PCTSUM < SITE*PROV1
         SITE*ALL
         ALL*PROV1
         ALL>
```

Why Did the WEIGHT Statement Have No Effect?

The WEIGHT statement tells PROC TABULATE to produce weighted SUM, MEAN, or STD statistics for the analysis variables in the TABLE statement. The value used for weighting statistics is stored in the variable specified in the WEIGHT statement. The FREQ statement tells TABULATE to treat each observation as multiple identical observations. The frequency of each observation is stored in the variable specified in the FREQ statement.

The WEIGHT statement for PROC TABULATE differs from the WEIGHT statement for PROC FREQ. If you want to achieve the effect of the WEIGHT statement in PROC FREQ in PROC TABULATE, use the FREQ statement instead.

When Is a Table Too Large?

If you are printing a very large table, you might encounter a message like this one:

```
A COLUMN DIMENSION CROSSING PRODUCED MORE THAN 32767 COLUMNS
IN THE TABLE AT LINE nn.
```

This message occurs when a table has too many values for class variables in a single dimension.† For example, if you code this TABULATE step

```
PROC TABULATE;
    CLASS DEPT DIVISION SSN;
    TABLE DEPT*DIVISION*SSN;
RUN;
```

and the data set has 8 values each for DEPT and DIVISION and 600 values for SSN, TABULATE produces the error message listed above. The number of columns in this case is 8*8*600 or 38,400. To overcome this situation, you can

- evaluate whether you really want to print each value produced by the TABLE statement. You might want to group values for a variable into a smaller number of classes.
- rearrange the TABLE statement so the variable that has the largest number of values is the only variable in a dimension. For example, the TABLE statement above could be rewritten as

    ```
    TABLE DEPT*DIVISION,SSN;
    ```

    This only works if the variable has fewer than 32,767 values.
- split the data and produce several tables.

---

† TABULATE prints similar messages for row and page dimensions.

References

Ott, L. (1977), *An Introduction to Statistical Methods and Data Analysis*, North Scituate, Mass.: Duxbury Press.

Snedecor, G.W. and Cochran, W.C. (1967), *Statistical Methods*, 6th Edition, Ames, Iowa: Iowa State University Press.

Index

Proofreading and text entry support are performed in the **Technical Writing Department** by **Amy E. Ball**, **Gina A. Eatmon**, **Rebecca A. Fritz**, **Lisa K. Hunt**, **Caroline T. Powell**, **Beth L. Puryear**, **Drew T. Saunders**, **W. Robert Scott**, and **Harriet J. Watts** under the supervision of **David D. Baggett**. **Gigi Hassan** is index editor.

Production is performed in the **Graphic Arts Department**. Composition was provided by **Blanche W. Phillips**. Text composition programming was provided by **Craig R. Sampson**.

Creative Services artist **Lisa N. Clements** provided illustrations under the direction of **Jennifer A. Davis**.